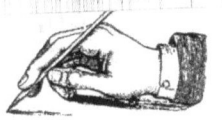

Guide to the Historical Records of Oklahoma, Revised Edition

Bradford Koplowitz

HERITAGE BOOKS
2007

HERITAGE BOOKS
AN IMPRINT OF HERITAGE BOOKS, INC.

Books, CDs, and more—Worldwide

For our listing of thousands of titles see our website
at
www.HeritageBooks.com

Published 2007 by
HERITAGE BOOKS, INC.
Publishing Division
65 East Main Street
Westminster, Maryland 21157-5026

Copyright © 1997 Bradford Koplowitz

Other books by the author:
Guide to the Historical Records of Oklahoma
Guide to the Historical Records of Oklahoma (Revised Edition)
The Kaw Indian Census and Allotments

All rights reserved. No part of this book may be reproduced or transmitted in any form or by any means, electronic or mechanical, including photocopying, recording or by any information storage and retrieval system without written permission from the author, except for the inclusion of brief quotations in a review.

International Standard Book Number: 978-0-7884-0730-7

TABLE OF CONTENTS

PREFACE TO THE REVISED EDITION xi

INTRODUCTION xiii

MAP OF OKLAHOMA COUNTY AND COUNTY SEATS xv

COUNTIES

Adair	1
Alfalfa	2
Atoka	5
Beaver	6
Beckham	8
Blaine	10
Bryan	13
Caddo	15
Canadian	17
Carter	20
Cherokee	21
Choctaw	23
Cimarron	26
Cleveland	29
Coal	31
Comanche	36
Cotton	43
Craig	45
Creek	47
Custer	49
Delaware	50
Dewey	51
Ellis	53
Garfield	55
Garvin	57
Grady	59
Grant	60
Greer	62
Harmon	64

COUNTIES (continued)

Harper 66
Haskell 67
Hughes 69
Jackson 71
Jefferson 72
Johnston 75
Kay 76
Kingfisher 80
Kiowa 81
Latimer 83
LeFlore 84
Lincoln 86
Logan 90
Love 92
McClain 94
McCurtain 98
McIntosh 99
Major 100
Marshall 102
Mayes 103
Murray 105
Muskogee 106
Noble 108
Nowata 113
Okfuskee 114
Oklahoma 116
Okmulgee 119
Osage 120
Ottawa 123
Pawnee 125
Payne 127
Pittsburg 129
Pontotoc 133
Pottawatomie 134
Pushmataha 136
Roger Mills 137
Rogers 139
Seminole 141
Sequoyah 143
Stephens 144
Texas 146
Tillman 152
Tulsa 154
Wagoner 156
Washington 157

iv

COUNTIES (continued)

Washita 158
Woods 162
Woodward 164

CITIES AND TOWNS

Ada 167
Altus 167
Alva 168
Anadarko 168
Antlers 168
Ardmore 168
Atoka 168
Bartlesville 169
Bethany 169
Bixby 169
Blackwell 169
Bristow 169
Broken Arrow 170
Broken Bow 170
Chandler 170
Checotah 170
Chickasha 171
Choctaw 171
Claremore 171
Clinton 171
Collinsville 171
Cordell 172
Coweta 172
Cushing 172
Del City 172
Dewey 172
Dickson 173
Drumright 173
Duncan 173
Durant 173
Edmond 173
El Reno 173
Elk City 174
Enid 175
Eufaula 176
Fairview 176
Frederick 177
Grove 177

CITIES AND TOWNS (continued)

Guthrie 177
Guymon 179
Healdton 179
Henryetta 179
Hobart 180
Holdenville 180
Hollis 180
Idabel 180
Jenks 180
Kingfisher 181
Lawton 181
Lone Grove 181
McAlester 181
McLoud 182
Madill 182
Mangum 182
Marlow 182
Miami 182
Midwest City 183
Moore 183
Muskogee 183
Mustang 184
Newcastle 184
Nichols Hills 184
Noble 184
Norman 184
Nowata 185
Okemah 185
Oklahoma City 185
Okmulgee 186
Owasso 187
Pauls Valley 187
Pawhuska 187
Perry 187
Pocola 188
Ponca City 188
Poteau 189
Pryor 189
Purcell 189
Sallisaw 189
Sand Springs 189
Sapulpa 190
Sayre 190
Seminole 190
Shawnee 190

CITIES AND TOWNS (continued)

Skiatook 191
Spencer 191
Stillwater 192
Stroud 192
Tahlequah 192
Tecumseh 193
Tonkawa 193
The Village 193
Tishomingo 193
Tulsa 194
Tuttle 194
Vinita 195
Wagoner 195
Warr Acres 195
Watonga 195
Weatherford 195
Wewoka 196
Wilburton 196
Woodward 196
Yukon 197

GENERAL REPOSITORIES

Oklahoma Department of Libraries, State Archives Division

Boards of County Commissioners 199

Oklahoma Department of Libraries, State Records Center

Cleveland County 199

Oklahoma Historical Society, Archives and Manuscripts Division

Counties:

Comanche 199
Greer 200
Johnston 202
Kiowa 204
Logan 206
Muskogee 206
Osage 206
Payne 207
Pottawatomie 207

GENERAL REPOSITORIES (continued)

    Swanson 211

    Normal Institute Records (Edmond, Oklahoma) 212

State Election Board, Oklahoma Museum of Election History

    Counties:

        Adair 212
        Blaine 212
        Carter 212
        Choctaw 212
        Cleveland 212
        Coal 212
        Creek 212
        Custer 213
        Dewey 213
        Ellis 213
        Garfield 213
        Grant 213
        Greer 213
        Kingfisher 213
        Latimer 213
        LeFlore 213
        Lincoln 214
        Major 214
        Marshall 214
        Mayes 214
        Murray 214
        Muskogee 214
        Noble 214
        Nowata 214
        Pawnee 215
        Payne 215
        Pontotoc 215
        Pottawatomie 215
        Roger Mills 215
        Rogers 215
        Sequoyah 215
        Tillman 215
        Wagoner 215
        Washita 216

GENERAL REPOSITORIES (continued)

University of Oklahoma, Western History Collections

Fairland (City Records Collection) 216
Fort Gibson (Records of the First National Bank) 217
Logan (County Road Records Collection) 217
Miami (City Records Collection) 217
Nowata (County Records Collection) 217
Quapaw (City Records Collection) 217
Shumard, Evelyn H., Collection
    (Records of Town of Sapulpa) 218
Welch (Town Records Collection) 218
Womack, John, Collection
    (Records of Cleveland County) 218

PREFACE TO THE REVISED EDITION

The Guide to the Historical Records of Oklahoma, Revised Edition lists public records through 1920 for the county offices of Assessor, Board of County Commissioners, County Clerk, Court Clerk, Election Board, Sheriff, Superintendent of Schools, and Treasurer in all seventy-seven counties throughout Oklahoma. Municipal records for cities and towns with over 5,000 in population or of historic significance are also included. In addition, the Guide contains listings of public records stored in historical societies, museums, public libraries, and special collections. This new edition differs from the 1990 version because it contains new and expanded holdings statements for many offices, as well as format changes designed to make it easier to use.

The purpose of the Guide is to identify records from the territorial and early statehood periods that still exist. Such records have pertinence to matters such as birth and death, marriage and divorce, land ownership, litigation, schools and students, and the development of cities and towns. Thus, the Guide is primarily of use to researchers in the fields of genealogy and local history.

As before, this edition primarily relied upon a survey of county and municipal officials through contacts made by letter and telephone. Survey responses were transcribed nearly word for word with only minor editing changes. The holdings statements appear to be fairly complete when compared to the on-site surveys which were undertaken. Although the survey only polled records through 1920, records past that date, which respondents described in their questionnaires, were included in the Guide.

An important change in Oklahoma's county governments occurred in 1994 with the dissolution of the office of the Superintendent of Schools. The records of this office remain in the county courthouses under the authority of the County Clerk. However, in some counties the records have not been moved and are maintained by the Board of County Commissioners.

To write to a county or municipal officer, consult the addresses of county seats and municipalities which precede each listing. A typical address would be Pontotoc County Court Clerk, County Courthouse, Ada, OK 74820, or Muskogee City Clerk, City Hall, Muskogee, OK 74401.

As always, thanks go to Don DeWitt, Shirley Clark, and Nancy Koplowitz for their steadfast support.

INTRODUCTION

In my positions as Assistant Curator of the University of Oklahoma's Western History Collections from October 1986 to the present, and as Head of the Oklahoma State Archives Division of the Oklahoma Department of Libraries from 1982-1986, it has become obvious that a finding aid was needed to access Oklahoma's historical records. Patrick J. Blessing's Oklahoma: Records and Archives (Tulsa, Oklahoma: University of Tulsa Publications, 1978) is a helpful tool for genealogists but only covers vital-statistic-type records. Other works such as Mary M. O'Brien's Oklahoma Genealogical Research (Sand Springs, Oklahoma: M. O'Brien Bookshop, 1986), and Jean C. Brown's Oklahoma Research: The Twin Territories (Sapulpa, Oklahoma: n.p., 1975) delineate general sources of genealogical data but do not contain inventories of records.

The Works Progress Administration (WPA) with its Historical Records Survey of 1935 to 1943 attempted to compile a comprehensive listing of records for Oklahoma's counties and municipalities. However, the WPA published inventories for just eleven of Oklahoma's seventy-seven counties, and produced unpublished field forms for only sixty-four municipalities. Furthermore, since the WPA's survey is nearly fifty years old, its findings are largely outmoded because many of the records no longer exist.

A guide to records at the county and municipal levels would locate resources which document the life cycle of people from birth to death, and preserve information concerning significant life events such as marriage and divorce, land ownership and the passing of property to heirs. Records also provide evidence of the history of litigations, the growth and decline of places, and the development of local governments. Thus, a guide to county and municipal records would have significance for furthering research in such fields as genealogy, regional history, sociology and political science.

With support from the Oklahoma Foundation for the Humanities and the University of Oklahoma, we undertook to survey public records through 1920 of all county governments, and all municipal governments of towns with over 5,000 in population or of historic significance. In the winter of 1988, we conducted an on-site pilot survey of records in Cleveland County and the city of Norman. Results of this study were evaluated as part of the development of a statewide survey instrument (questionnaire).

On March 1, 1989, questionnaires were mailed to 106 city clerks, and to the following offices in each of Oklahoma's seventy-seven counties: Assessor, Board of County Commissioners, County Clerk, Court Clerk, Election Board, Sheriff, Superintendent of Schools, and Treasurer. A second questionnaire was mailed on

May 15 with extensive follow-up contacts by telephone and letter throughout the summer. On-site visits were kept to a minimum due to a limited budget.

Five hundred ninety-nine out of 616 county offices and ninety-seven out of 106 city clerks responded to the survey. In addition, if a respondent indicated that public records were stored at another repository such as a local historical society, museum or public library, we sent that repository a questionnaire. Lastly, we surveyed general repositories such as the State Historical Society to find out which county and municipal records were in their custody.

The WPA was able to conduct on-site inspections by trained auditors, whereas our survey was "impersonal" due to its reliance on mail and telephone contacts. Therefore, we cannot attest to its absolute accuracy or completeness. On the other hand, a Guide to the Historical Records of Oklahoma provides for the first time a general accounting of Oklahoma's historical records in one published work. This will enable researchers to infer which records should be in the custody of local officials. For instance, since most of the County Superintendents of Schools have School Enumeration Records (Census), it would behoove a researcher interested in such data to make inquiry of County Superintendents who did not include census records as part of their response.

The Guide descriptions were taken verbatim from the survey instrument forms with only minor editing changes. This was done in a conscious effort to signify records in the same way as their keepers. Although the survey was only intended to elicit listings of records dated before 1921, numerous respondents decided to include records of a more recent origin. Offices which are not mentioned in the Guide failed to respond to the survey. In order to write to an office, please note the addresses of county seats and municipalities which are included in the place name headings in the text.

The author wishes to thank the Oklahoma Foundation for the Humanities and the University of Oklahoma for financial support; Donald DeWitt for his sage counsel; Sharron Ashton and Jan Skelton for their encouragement and advice; Shirley Clark and Mary McClain for their skillful word processing; and Nancy Koplowitz for her optimism and support. In addition, this project would not have been completed without the assistance of Oklahoma's county and municipal officers, and the student workers at the Western History Collections.

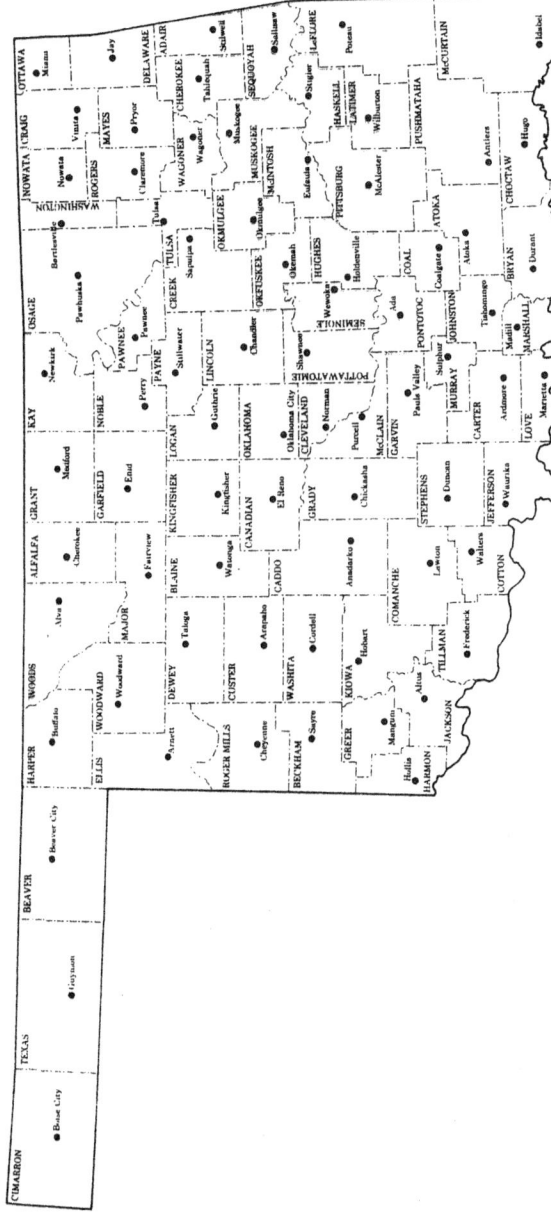

J. W. Morris Collection Map Number 10
Western History Collections, University of Oklahoma Libraries

COUNTIES

Adair (Stilwell, OK 74960)

Assessor

   None (courthouse burned in 1929).

Board of County Commissioners

   Commissioners' Journals. Minutes of proceedings, includes details of matters discussed, actions taken, names of parties and all dates, chronological, no index, 2 books, 1907-1920.

County Clerk

   Allotment Books. South end of Adair County (volume one), north end of Adair County (volume two), by legal description, 2 volumes, 1906-07.

   Deed Record Books. By legal description, approximately 60 volumes, 1907-32 (some years missing).

Court Clerk

   Probate. Index, dockets and cases, chronological, alphabetical (indexes), 3 volumes (indexes), 16 volumes (dockets), 1907 to date.

   Civil. Index, case records, dockets and civil journals, chronological, alphabetical (indexes), 5 volumes (indexes), 21 volumes (dockets), 19 volumes (civil journals), 1907 to date.

   Divorce. Index, case records and dockets, chronological, alphabetical (indexes), 8 volumes (dockets), 1907 to date (before 1921 listed with civil cases).

   Marriage. Index and marriage records, chronological, alphabetical, 3 volumes (indexes), 38 volumes (records), 1907 to date.

   Criminal. Dockets, cases and index, chronological, alphabetical, 13 volumes (dockets), 3 volumes (indexes), 1907 to date.

ADAIR
COUNTIES

Juvenile (confidential). Dockets and cases, chronological, alphabetical, 4 volumes (dockets), 1907 to date.

Mental Health (confidential). Dockets and cases, chronological, alphabetical, 5 volumes (dockets), 1907 to date.

Adoption (confidential). Dockets and cases, chronological, alphabetical, 2 volumes (dockets), 1907 to date.

Election Board

Registrations. Race, color, politics, registration certificate number, name, school district, date of registration, age, residence, occupation, no arrangement, 1 box (sheets), 1916-34.

Sheriff

None.

Superintendent of Schools

None.

Treasurer

None.

Alfalfa (Cherokee, OK 73728)

Assessor

Records stored in courthouse basement (inaccessible).

Board of County Commissioners

None.

County Clerk

Final Receipt Record. Exact copies of receipt records on real property, date and number of instrument, names of grantor and grantee, legal description of property, date and time filed, chronological, indexed alphabetically, 6 volumes, 1898-1914.

COUNTIES   ALFALFA

Patent Record. Exact copies of patent records on real property, date and number of instrument, names of grantor and grantee, legal description of property, date and time filed, chronological, indexed alphabetically, 12 volumes, 1896-1904.

Deed Record. Exact copies of deed records on real property, date and number of instrument, names of grantor and grantee, legal description of property, date and time filed, chronological, indexed alphabetically, 71 volumes, 1895-1920.

Mortgage Record. Exact copies of mortgage records on real property, date and number of instrument, names of mortgagor and mortgagee, amount and conditions, legal description of property, date and time filed, chronological, indexed alphabetically, 45 volumes, 1895-1920.

Miscellaneous Record. Exact copies of miscellaneous records on real property, etc., date and number of instrument, names of grantor and grantee, legal description of property, date and time filed, chronological, indexed alphabetically, 36 volumes, 1892-1920.

Grantor Record. Exact copies of grantor and grantee records, date and number of instrument, names of grantor to grantee, legal description of property, date and time filed, chronological, indexed alphabetically, 3 volumes, 1895-1920.

Grantee Record. Exact copies of grantee and grantor records, date and number of instrument, names of grantee to grantor, legal description of property, date and time filed, chronological, indexed alphabetically, 3 volumes, 1895-1920.

Mortgagor Index Record. Exact copies of mortgagor to mortgagee records, date and number of instrument, names of mortgagor and mortgagee, legal description of property, date and time filed, chronological, indexed alphabetically, 2 volumes, 1895-1920.

Mortgagee Index Record. Exact copies of mortgagee to mortgagor records, date and number of instrument, names of mortgagee and mortgagor, legal description of property, date and time filed, chronological, indexed alphabetically, 2 volumes, 1895-1920.

Numerical Index Tract Records of Cities and Towns, Township and Range. Date of instrument, name of grantor and grantee, book and page, and legal description, chronological, indexed alphabetically, 33 volumes, 1893-1920.

Court Clerk

Probate. Index, dockets and cases, chronological, 6 volumes, 1907-1920.

Civil. Index, dockets and cases, chronological, 5 volumes, 1907-1920.

ALFALFA

Felony. Index, dockets and cases, chronological, 4 volumes, 1907-1920.

Misdemeanor. Index, dockets and cases, chronological, 4 volumes, 1907-1920.

Marriage. Application, marriage license and index, recorded in books, chronological, 4 volumes, 1907-1920.

Small Claims. Index, dockets and cases, chronological, 3 volumes, 1907-1920.

Election Board

Records stored in the Alfalfa County Historical Society Museum, Cherokee, Oklahoma.

Historical Society Museum, Alfalfa County

Tax Roll Books. Chronological, 1907-1967.

School Warrant Register Books. Early 1900's to 1960's.

County Warrant Books.

Old Delinquent Tax Books.

Sheriff

None.

Superintendent of Schools

School District Plat Books. Establishment of schools, annexations, and consolidations in Alfalfa County and Woods County, legal descriptions, by numerical order of school district and chronological order, 1 volume, 1895-1920.

Register of Teachers Employed. Name of teacher, school district, number of months taught, annual and monthly salary, etc., alphabetical order, 1 volume, 1907-20.

School Enumeration Record (Census). Full name of student, date of birth, name of parent or guardian, etc., by school district and name of student, 8 volumes, 1912-1920.

COUNTIES *ATOKA*

Treasurer

All records prior to 1921 stored in the Alfalfa County Historical Society Museum, Cherokee, Oklahoma.

Atoka (Atoka, OK 74525)

Assessor

None.

Board of County Commissioners

Minutes (stored in the office of the County Clerk). Proceedings of meetings of the county commissioners, chronological, 8 volumes, 1937 to date.

Confederate Memorial Museum (Atoka County Historical Society)

Zweigel Funeral Home Records. Burial records, some containing names of decedent's parents, birth dates, ages, and place of burial, chronological order with alphabetical index, 10 volumes, July 1912-October 1944.

Canvass of Tombstones, County Cemeteries. Information copied from tombstones, alphabetical order by cemetery, 1 loose-leaf volume, 1856-1984 (also contains information on thirty abandoned burial sites found on family farms and other locations not normally used for burials).

Canvass of Tombstones, Atoka City Cemetery (Westview). Information copied from tombstones, arranged in order of stone's placement in cemetery, 1 loose-leaf volume, 1877-1986.

Register of Prisoners, Atoka County, Oklahoma. Lists prisoners booked into Atoka County Jail, chronological, 1 volume, August 1922-December 1932 and September 1937-June 1941.

Register of Prisoners, Atoka County, Oklahoma. Lists prisoners booked into Atoka County Jail, chronological, 1 volume, July 1941-July 1951.

Note: Funeral home records may be found at the Atoka Funeral Home, Atoka, Oklahoma, and the Atoka Public Library maintains a copy of the county cemetery records.

ATOKA

County Clerk

Land Records and Mortgages. Legal descriptions, 496 volumes, time filed, alphabetical order, 1907-1920.

Election Board

No records prior to 1921 with the exception of some early voter registrations and election results stored in the office of the County Clerk.

Sheriff

None.

Superintendent of Schools

Scholastic Census Records. Includes name of parent, name of student, date of birth, place of birth, grades, sex, disability (if any), address, occupation of parent, name of tribe (if Indian), etc., chronological, 1 book for each school district per year, approximately 100 books per year, 1912-1970.

Register of School Warrants. Checks issued as payment, chronological, by school district, 1 volume, 1912-1970s.

Treasurer

Tax Rolls (stored in courthouse basement with limited access). Property owners and land descriptions, chronological, hundreds of books, ca. 1907 to date.

Beaver (Beaver City, OK 73932)

Assessor

None.

Board of County Commissioners

Minutes (stored in the office of the County Clerk). Proceedings of meetings of county commissioners, chronological, 3 books, 1890-1920.

County Clerk

Deeds. Copies of deeds, patents, receipts, indexes (grantor-grantee, 3 volumes), chronological and alphabetical, 50 volumes, 1892-1920.

Mortgages. Copies of mortgages, release of mortgages, assignments of mortgages, indexes (grantor-grantee, 3 volumes), chronological and alphabetical, 52 volumes, 1897-1920.

Oil and Gas Records. Oil and gas leases, mineral deeds, assignments, releases of leases, chronological and alphabetical, 1 volume, 1917-1920.

Miscellaneous Records. Final decrees, judgments, agreements and anything not covered in the preceding record series, indexes (grantor-grantee, 1 volume), chronological and alphabetical, 5 volumes, 1890-1920.

Court Clerk

Civil. Journal entries of daily proceedings, number of cases, names of attorneys and judges, some indexes, 14 volumes, 1890-1921.

Probate. Journal entries of daily proceedings, number of cases, names of attorneys, judges and court clerks, some indexes, 14 volumes, 1891-1921.

Criminal. Charges, number of cases, proceedings, some indexes, 8 volumes, 1902-1914.

Marriage License. General, indexed, 5 volumes, 1890 to date.

Note: Some records are stored in the Texas County Courthouse, Guymon, OK.

Election Board.

None.

Sheriff.

None.

Superintendent of Schools

Examination of Applicants for Teachers' Certificates. Name of applicant, address, age, number of weeks of experience as teacher, test grades, date of issue and expiration, by date of examination, 1 volume, 1891-1907.

School Census Records. Name of child, date of birth, name of parents, school district, books for each district, 1913-1920.

BEAVER *COUNTIES*

Year Book. School census, assessed valuation, school district officers, teachers, school term, appropriations and levy, report of pupils, miscellaneous, by school district number, 3 volumes, 1918-1920.

Treasurer

Tax Rolls of Ad Valorem Taxes. Assessed value for real and personal property, name of owner, name of person paying tax, amount paid, rural areas by legal description (township, range and section), towns in block and lot order, personal property chronological and alphabetical, 1891- (some years missing).

Beckham (Sayre, OK 73662)

Assessor

Assessment Rolls. Personal property listings of owners and values, real estate legal descriptions, owners and values, personal property by school district and alphabetical name, real estate by legal description (section, township and range), 81 books, 1907-1920.

Board of County Commissioners

None (records stored in the office of the County Clerk).

County Clerk

Patents (Transcribed). Copies of patents, book and pages, description, dated and time filed, numerical and alphabetical, 3 volumes, 1900-1906.

Deeds (Transcribed). Copies of deeds, book and pages, description, dated and time filed, numerical and alphabetical, 10 volumes, 1901-1907.

Mortgages (Transcribed). Copies of mortgages, book and pages, description, dated and time filed, numerical and alphabetical, 10 volumes, 1900-1907.

Patents. Copies of patents, book and pages, description, dated and time filed, numerical and alphabetical, 6 volumes, 1907-1920.

Deeds. Copies of deeds, book and pages, description, dated and time filed, numerical and alphabetical, 34 volumes, 1907-1920.

Mortgages. Copies of mortgages, book and pages, description, dated and time filed, numerical and alphabetical, 33 volumes, 1907-1920.

COUNTIES *BECKHAM*

Miscellaneous. Copies of miscellaneous, book and pages, description, dated and time filed, numerical and alphabetical, 20 volumes, 1907-1920.

Transcribed Numerical Index. General information of an instrument, 1 volume, 1900-1907.

Numerical Indexes. General information of an instrument, 22 volumes, 1907 to date.

Cemetery Book. Description, book and pages, dated and time filed, 1 volume, 1907 to date.

Plat Book of Government Surveys. Copies of maps, 1 volume, 1907.

Plats of Towns or Cities in Beckham County. Copies of plats, description, book and pages, dated and time filed, stored in plat cabinet, 1900 to date.

Court Clerk

Probate. Index, dockets and case files, microfilm, chronological, 15 volumes, 1907 to date.

Civil. Index, dockets, case files and judgments, microfilm, general index, chronological, 36 volumes, 1907 to date.

Divorce. Index, dockets, case files and decrees, microfilm, general index, chronological, 11 volumes, 1907 to date.

Felony (Crf). Index, dockets and case files, microfilm, chronological, 8 volumes, 1907 to date.

Misdemeanor (Crm). Index, dockets and case files, judgment and sentence signed by judge, microfilm, chronological, 25 volumes, 1907 to date.

Marriage License. Index and dockets, chronological, 45 volumes, 1907 to date.

Small Claim. Index, dockets and case files, chronological, 7 volumes, 1969 to date.

Traffic. Index and case files, chronological.

Adoption (confidential). Index, case files and dockets, chronological, 4 volumes.

Passports.

BECKHAM   COUNTIES

   Notary.

   Bingo License.

   Juvenile (confidential). Index, case files and dockets, chronological, 4 volumes.

   Mental Health (confidential). Index, case files and dockets, chronological, 2 volumes.

   Beverage License.

Election Board

   Elections. Election returns, chronological, 1948 to date.

Sheriff

   None.

Superintendent of Schools

   School Enumeration Records (Census). Name of student, date of birth, etc., chronological, by school district, hundreds of books, 1915-1968.

   Teacher Employment Records. Information about teachers, chronological, alphabetical, 3 volumes, 1909-1955.

Treasurer

   Tax Rolls (stored in warehouse). Legal owner of property in Beckham County, 1907 to date.

Blaine (Watonga, OK 73772)

Assessor

   Assessment Rolls. Acreage of landowner, by school districts and alphabetical, volume unclear (some destroyed), 1900 to date.

Board of County Commissioners

   Proceedings and Road Records of the County Commissioners. 1892 to date.

COUNTIES *BLAINE*

County Clerk

Minutes. Proceedings of meetings of the county commissioners, 1890s to date.

Deed Records. Copies of deeds including description of property, book and page, and date and time of filing, chronological, 94 volumes, 1892-1958.

Mortgage Records. Copies of mortgages including description of property, book and page, and date and time of filing, chronological, 73 volumes, 1895-1958.

Oil and Gas Lease Records. Copies of oil and gas leases including description of property, book and page, and date and time of filing, chronological, 43 volumes, 1917-1958.

Patent Records. Homestead patents including inherited land deeds, list description of property, book and page, and date and time of filing, chronological and alphabetical, 6 volumes, 1895-1958.

Final Receipt Records. Receipt records for homesteads, description of property received, book and page, and date and time of filing, chronological, 2 volumes, 1895-1914.

Release of Mortgage Records. Copies of releases of mortgages, description of property, book and page of original mortgage, book and page, and date and time of filing, chronological, 17 volumes, 1903-1958.

Cemetery Book. Index of cemetery deeds, listed by cemetery, block and lot, 1 volume, late 1800s to present.

Townsite Record. "C" County records, including trustee's deeds and mortgages, lists description of property, book and page, and date and time of filing, chronological, 1 volume, 1892-1894.

Miscellaneous Record Books. Include documents not listed in other books prior to 1958 and all documents after 1958, lists property description when applicable, book and page, and date and time of filing, chronological, 725 volumes, 1892 to present.

Plat Books. Original plats of towns, additions, sub-divisions, cemeteries, etc., book and page, and date and time of filing, 3 volumes, 1892 to present.

Government Survey Books. Maps of government surveys for each section, township and range, arranged by township and range, 1 volume, 1873.

Military Discharge Records. Copies of military discharge papers, book and page, and date and time of filing, 7 volumes, 1919 to present.

School Enumeration Records. Name of student, date of birth, etc., by school district, chronological, hundreds of volumes, late 1800s-1967.

Teacher Employment Records. Information about teachers employed by Blaine County Schools, chronological, 4 volumes, 1892-1972.

Court Clerk

Marriage Records. Marriage applications and marriage licenses recorded, indexed by name, 9 volumes (1892-1920), 1892 to date.

Probate Records. Probate of estates filed for the county, indexed by name of the deceased, 4 volumes (1892-1920), 1892 to date.

Criminal Records. Felony and misdemeanor records filed in the county, indexed by name of the defendant, 4 volumes (1892-1920), 1892 to date.

Civil Records. Cases filed in the county, include name of attorney, judgments and orders of court, indexed by name of plaintiff and defendant, several books, 1892 to date.

Divorce Records. Divorces filed in the county, indexed by name of plaintiff and defendant, filed in civil appearance dockets, several books, 1892 to date.

Election Board

Election Register. Name, school district number, registration date, town, occupation, race, politics, registration certificate number (voting information begins in 1938), by precinct name and identification number, 1 book ("Flynn Number 13"), 1916-1940.

Sheriff

Jail Book. Name and address, chronological, 2 volumes, 1900 to date.

Superintendent of Schools

Scholastic Census Report. Name of each school age child living in district, race, sex, date of birth, name of parents and signature, enumerator's signature and date, numerical by school district number and chronological, 1904-1967 (new listing as School Enumeration Records under County Clerk).

COUNTIES *BRYAN*

Record of School District Officers. School board officers (director, clerk and treasurer) for each school district in county, term of office, numerical by school district number and chronological, 3 volumes, 1910 to date.

Employed Teacher Register. Teacher's name, school district number, length of contract, some salary amounts and certification held, numerical by school district number and chronological, 4 volumes, 1893-1973 (new listing as Teacher Employment Records under County Clerk).

School District Plats. Plats of each school district, some detachments, attachments and dates in later years, numerical by school district number, 2 volumes, 1894 to date.

Treasurer

Tax Rolls (stored in the Ferguson Museum, Watonga, OK). Chronological, 1898-1930.

Bryan (Durant, OK 74701)

Assessor

None.

Board of County Commissioners

None.

County Clerk

Numerical Land Index. For sections, townships and ranges, numerical, 5 books, 1903 to date.

Deed Index. Direct and indirect, book and page to find recorded instruments, alphabetical, 6 books, 1903-1920.

Mortgage Index. Direct and indirect, book and page to find mortgages, alphabetical, 5 books, 1903-1920.

Patents. Allotment and town lot patents, allotment patents for years 1904-1906, town lot patents for years 1903-1940, by instrument, 2 books, 1903-1940.

Physicians' Certificates. Certificates to practice, alphabetical, 1 book, 1917 to date.

BRYAN *COUNTIES*

Military Discharges. DD214 (record of service), alphabetical, 14 books, 1919 to date.

Court Clerk

Probate. Index, dockets and cases, chronological, 4 volumes, 1912-1920.

Civil. Index, dockets and cases, chronological, 8 volumes, 1902-1920.

Felony. Index, dockets and some cases, chronological, 2 volumes, December 17, 1907-1920.

Marriage License - Indian Territory. Index and dockets, chronological, 2 volumes, 1902-1907.

Marriage License. Index and dockets, chronological, 12 volumes, 1908- 1920.

Election Board

None (no records prior to 1950).

Sheriff
None.

Superintendent of Schools

School Enumeration Records (Census). Name of student, date of birth, etc., chronological, by school district, 57 books, 1918-1967.

Teachers' Employment Records. Information about teachers, chronological, alphabetical, 3 books, 1913-1985.

School District Boundary Records. Consolidations, annexations, etc., 2 books, 1940 to date.

Treasurer

Tax Rolls.

Note: Additional records stored in the Bryan County Heritage Association Research Library, Calera, OK.

COUNTIES CADDO

Caddo (Anadarko, OK 73005)

Assessor

Assessment Rolls. Legal description and values, personal property and values, chronological and alphabetical, 19 volumes, 1916-1919.

Board of County Commissioners

Minutes (stored in the office of the County Clerk). Information regarding all business attended to including contracts, resolutions, etc., chronological, approximately 5 books, 1901-1920.

County Clerk

Townsite Certificate. Exact copies of town lot certificate records from the Commissioner of the General Land Office, date of instrument, name of purchaser, legal description and date of filing, indexed, 1 volume, 1901-1910.

County Patent. Exact copies of patents issued by the United States Government, name of purchaser, legal description, date of instrument and date of filing, indexed, 5 volumes, 1903-1912.

Release and Assignment. Exact copies of release and assignment of mortgages on real property, date of instrument, book and page of mortgage releasing and or assigning, legal description, and date and time of filing, indexed, 68 volumes, 1902-1958.

Mortgage. Exact copies of mortgages on real property, date of instrument, names of mortgagee and mortgagor, amount, terms, legal description, book and page and date of filing, indexed, 163 volumes, 1902-1958.

Trustees' Deeds. Exact copies of deeds from trustee of town to purchaser, legal description (lots and blocks), date of filing, book and page, indexed, 5 volumes, 1901-1926.

Town Patent Books. Exact copies of patents from the United States Government to purchaser, lot and block, date of instrument, date of filing, book and page, indexed, 1 volume, 1902-1910.

Deed. Exact copies of deeds, date of filing, book and page, grantor, grantee, legal description, indexed, 1901 to date.

CADDO *COUNTIES*

Court Clerk

> <u>District, Civil</u>. Appearance dockets and recording journals, style of case, case number, type of action, all pleadings and instruments, attorney of record, court costs, court minutes, date of all filings, filed case number index (alphabetical), September 1901 to date.
>
> <u>Probate</u>. Appearance dockets and recording journals, style of case, case number, type of action, all pleadings and instruments, attorney of record, court costs, court minutes, date of all filings, filed case number index (alphabetical), September 1901 to date.
>
> <u>Marriage Records</u>. Names of parties, resident information, ages of parties, date of application, date of marriage, place of marriage, names of witnesses, name of person who performed ceremony, alphabetical, chronological, 1901 to date.
>
> <u>Felony</u>. Appearance dockets and recording journals, style of case, case number, type of action, all pleadings and instruments, attorney of record, court costs, court minutes, date of all filings, alphabetical, 1901 to date.
>
> <u>Divorce, Paternity, Child Custody, Reciprocal Child Support</u>. Appearance dockets and recording journals, style of case, case number, type of action, all pleadings and instruments, attorney of record, court costs, court minutes, date of all filings, alphabetical, 1901 to date.

Election Board

> None (no records prior to 1952).

Superintendent of Schools

> <u>School Census Records</u>. Name of parents and students, date of birth, by school district and chronological, 5 filing cabinets, 1912-1968.
>
> <u>School Board Members</u>. Position and term of office, by school district, 1 book, 1901- ?.
>
> <u>School District Boundaries</u>. Record of changes in school district boundaries (annexations), arranged by school district, 3 books, 1901 to date.
>
> <u>Caddo County Educational Directories</u>. Lists of all school districts and teachers, arranged by school year, 1930 to date.

COUNTIES *CANADIAN*

Treasurer

None (no records prior to 1972).

Canadian (El Reno, OK 73036)

Assessor

None (records stored in the El Reno Carnegie Library, El Reno, OK).

Board of County Commissioners

None (all records stored in the office of the County Clerk).

County Clerk

Bond Register. Register of funding bond amounts and payments made, chronological, July 1891 - December 1895.

County Clerk's Open Market and Contract Purchase Record. Purchase order record, date of purchase order/requisition number, description of services or goods, quantity, amount, numerical by account/office, October 1915 - January 1916.

Equalization Board Record. Minutes of meetings, chronological, 1 volume, pages 1-11, June 1915 - June 1920.

Proceedings of Excise Board. Minutes of meetings, chronological, 1 volume, pages 1-169, July 1910 - June 1920.

Commissioners' Proceedings. Minutes of meetings, chronological, 5 volumes, June 11, 1890 - December 8, 1920.

Fee and Reception Record. Volumes "C" through "J", November 21, 1900 - December 30, 1920.

Grantor/Grantee Index. Alphabetical (chronological within), 5 volumes, September 1890 - December 1920.

Record of Physicians' Certificates. Registration of physicians by certificate, chronological, 2 volumes, July 1892 - July 1920.

Optometry Record. Certification of registered optometrists, alphabetical index in front, followed by chronological, August 1911.

CANADIAN *COUNTIES*

Indictment Record. Defendant's name, charge, filing date, chronological, 1 volume, April 1892 - December 1893.

Mortgagee Index/Mortgagor Index. Mortgagor, mortgagee, date of filing, date of instrument, book and page to be found, chronological with alphabetical index, 3 volumes, July 1890 -1920.

Oil and Gas Record. Exact copies of oil leases, assignments, releases, affidavits, waiver of mortgage liens, records prior to 1925 are in miscellaneous books 1-13, chronological, 47 volumes, January 1925 - January 1927.

Patent Book. Exact copies of patents from the United States Government to landowners, chronological, 7 volumes, October 1892 - December 1920.

Final Receipt. Exact copies of receipts for land, chronological, 2 volumes, August 1890 - August 1910.

Miscellaneous Record. Exact copies of oil and gas leases, assignments of leases, releases, affidavits, powers of attorney, final decrees of estates, final certificates of purchase, bills of sale, mortgages, contracts, chronological, 11 volumes, July 1890-1920.

Deed Record. Warranty deeds, quit claim deeds, chronological, 89 volumes, June 1890 - December 1920.

Mortgage Records and Mortgage Release Records. Mortgages, marginal release of mortgages and mortgage releases, chronological, 91 volumes, July 1890 - December 1920.

Court Clerk

General Index. Index books with case numbers, chronological, 5 volumes, 1892-1924.

District Court Journals. Books with copies of all instruments signed by judge, chronological, 23 volumes, 1892?-1921.

Probate. Administrator's record books (15 volumes), administrator's docket books (3 volumes), 1,039 cases, chronological, 18 volumes, 1890-1924.

Criminal. Appearance docket book, 4,055 cases, chronological, 7 volumes, 1890-1923.

Civil. Appearance docket books, 6,481 cases, chronological, 15 volumes, 1890-1922.

Marriage Record Books. Books of applications and licenses, chronological, 16 volumes, 1890-1924.

Guardianship. Guardianship appearance docket books (1 volume), guardianship record books (6 volumes), 456 cases, chronological, 7 volumes, 1890-1921.

Citizenship Record Books. Chronological, 4 volumes.

El Reno Carnegie Library, El Reno, OK 73036

Tax Roll. Original books, chronological, 1 book, 1909.

Marriage Records. Microfilm, chronological, 10 rolls, 1894-1941.

Naturalization. Microfilm, chronological, 2 rolls, 1890-1893.

Probate. Microfilm, chronological, 1894-1914.

Administration Records. Microfilm, chronological, 1905-1907.

Election Board

None.

Sheriff

None.

Superintendent of Schools

School District Enumeration Reports. School districts in county, family names, children's names, date of birth and sex, by year of record, school district number and alphabetical by families, 100 to 125 folders, 1907-1970.

Teacher Records. Names of teachers, years taught, districts where teachers taught, salaries of teachers, alphabetical, 1920s to date.

Teacher Contracts (incomplete). Salaries, district numbers, years taught, chronological and by school district number, 1920s to date.

List of County Superintendents for Canadian County. Superintendent's name, years in office, chronological, one page, 1890 to date.

Treasurer

    School District Warrant Register. Date, amount and to whom paid, by township and range, 1 volume, 1891-1893.

    School District Ledger. Taxes collected and disbursements, numerical by school district, 5 volumes, 1909-1922.

Carter (Ardmore, OK 73401)

Assessor

    None.

Board of County Commissioners

    None.

County Clerk

    Real Estate. Deeds, mortgages and miscellaneous, chronological and alphabetical, 100s of books, 1907 to date.

    Military Discharge Records. Copies of discharge papers, alphabetical, March 1919 to present.

    School District Enumeration Reports. Reports of school districts in Carter County including family names, names of students, date of birth and sex, arranged chronologically and by school district number, 1920s-1960s.

Court Clerk

    Marriage. Marriage licenses, indexed alphabetically in each docket, approximately 10 books, April 1895-1921.

    Criminal. Misdemeanor and felony, indexed alphabetically in each docket, approximately 5 books, April 1895-1921.

    Probate. Dockets and some files, approximately 5 books, April 1895-1921.

    Civil. Dockets and some files, indexed in dockets, approximately 5 books, April 1895-1921.

COUNTIES *CHEROKEE*

Ministers' Credentials. Recording of license or credential of ministers, indexed in front of each docket, approximately 2 books, April 1895-1921.

Naturalization. Docket book, unknown arrangement, 1 book, April 1895 -?.

Note: Some records are stored in the National Archives, Fort Worth Branch, Fort Worth, TX.

Election Board

None (no records prior to 1963).

Sheriff

Records stored in courthouse basement (inaccessible).

Superintendent of Schools

School Census Enumerations. Lists of children in households by school districts, alphabetical and chronological, 1910 to date (new listing as School District Enumeration Reports under County Clerk).

County Superintendent's Yearbook. List of teachers, board members, etc., for all school districts in county, chronological, 1917-1965.

Treasurer

None (records kept for 7 years).

Cherokee (Tahlequah, OK 74464)

Assessor

None (records kept for 15 years).

Board of County Commissioners

None.

County Clerk

Index to Deeds. Description of tract, grantee, grantor, date of filing, character of instrument, book and page, alphabetical, 2 volumes, 1907-1920.

21

Miscellaneous Index. Description of tract, grantee, grantor, date of filing, character of instrument, book and page, alphabetical, 2 volumes, 1907-1920.

Index to Mortgagors. Description of tract, grantee, grantor, date of filing, character of instrument, book and page, alphabetical, 2 volumes, 1907-1920.

Index to Lands. Book and page, remarks, grantor, grantee, date of instrument, kind of instrument, acres, chronological, 10 volumes, 1907-1920.

Soldiers' Discharge Record. Discharge information, alphabetical, 1 volume, 1919-1920.

Registration Record. Race, politics, registration certificate, name, school district, date of registration, age, residence, street number, occupation, chronological, 1 volume, 1916-1920.

Court Clerk

Civil - Divorce. Index, docket and cases, chronological, 36 volumes, 1907 to date.

Probate. Index, docket and cases, chronological, 16 volumes, 1907 to date.

Marriage Records. Docket books, chronological, 35 volumes, 1907 to date.

Felony. Index, docket and cases, chronological, 12 volumes, 1969 to date.

Misdemeanors. Index, docket and cases, chronological, 30 volumes, 1969 to date.

Traffic Tickets. Index, docket and cases, chronological, 1969 to date.

Election Board

None.

Sheriff

None.

Superintendent of Schools

School Enumeration Records (Census). Name of student, date of birth, etc., chronological by school district, 100s of books, 1913-1968.

COUNTIES *CHOCTAW*

Teachers' Employment Records. Information about teachers, chronological, alphabetical, 30-40 books, 1920s to date.

Deeds. School properties, chronological, files, 1920s to date.

Treasurer

None.

Choctaw (Hugo, OK 74743)

Assessor

Assessment Rolls. Parcel number, property description, market value, assessed value, exemptions, school district, land use code, name of owner and address of owner, and number of acres or lots, legal description by section, township and range, 1972 to present.

Personal Property Assessment Rolls. Name and address of owner of property, description of kind of personal property assessed, number of items, assessed value and exemptions, alphabetical by school district, 1972 to present.

Note: Assessment rolls from early statehood were given to the county historical society.

Board of County Commissioners

Deed Record. All land deeds, chronological, 40 volumes, 1907-1920.

Release and Assignment Records. Mortgage releases and assignments, chronological, 12 volumes, 1907-1920.

Mortgage Records. All mortgages, chronological, 33 volumes, 1907-1920.

Oil and Gas Leases. Chronological, 3 volumes, 1907-1920.

Record of Guardian Deeds. All deeds with guardianship, chronological, 1 volume, 1907-1920.

Dental Records. Dentist licenses, chronological, 1 volume, 1907-1920.

Register of Medical Certificates. Chronological, 1 volume, 1907-1920.

Registration Records. Register of electors, chronological, 1 volume, 1916-1920.

CHOCTAW COUNTIES

Fee Record. All fees recorded, chronological, 1 volume, 1907-1920.

Roll of Indian Lands. Legal descriptions of Indian lands, by township, range and section, 1 volume, 1902-?.

Allotment Patent. Indian allotment of lands, chronological, 2 volumes, 1903-1907.

Reception Record. All land and miscellaneous records, chronological, 8 volumes, 1907-1920.

District Records. Sale of timber, warranty deeds and chattel mortgages, chronological, books 1-25, 1903-1920.

Discharge Records. Soldiers' discharge records, chronological, 1 volume, 1919-1920.

Commissioners' Journal. Minutes of meetings, actions taken, dates, chronological, 3 volumes, 1907-1920.

Official Bond Record. Bonds, sheriff/judge, chronological, 1 volume, 1907-1920.

Physicians' Certificate Records. Certificates, chronological, 2 volumes, 1908-1920.

County Clerk

Land Records. Arranged by legal description, 1907-1921.

Court Clerk

Marriage. Name of persons, age, social security number/driver's license number, residence of both parties, and signature of parties, chronological, indexed alphabetically, 73 volumes, 1907 to present.

Civil. Quiet title, foreclosure, money judgment, name change, paternity suit, child support, forfeiture and seizure, petitions, summons, and court minutes, chronological, indexed alphabetically, 47 volumes, 1907 to present.

Divorce. Petition, summons, temporary orders, child custody, child support, property settlement, and divorce decree, chronological, indexed alphabetically, 6 volumes, 1907 to present.

Probate. Name of deceased, order appointing personal representative, appointment of administrator, notice to creditors, bond, publication, will, letters of testamentary, and order allowing final accounting, chronological, indexed alphabetically, 13 volumes, 1907 to present.

Felony. Information, arrest report, notice to appear, preliminary hearing, bind over, finding of facts, judgment and sentence, terms and conditions, and bond information, chronological, indexed alphabetically, 14 volumes, 1907 to present.

Misdemeanor. Information, arrest warrant, arrest report, arraignment, bond information, court appearance minutes, judgment and sentence, and terms and conditions, chronological, indexed alphabetically, 22 volumes, 1907 to present.

Beverage. Application, copy of sales tax permit, effective date, expiration date, legal description, and address, chronological.

Protective Order. Name of plaintiff and defendant, petition, court minute and order, alphabetical, 1 volume, 1993 to present.

Guardianship (confidential).

Mental Health (confidential).

Adoption (confidential).

Traffic. Defendant, age, height, address, telephone number, charge, and name of officer, chronological and alphabetical, 1974 to present.

Election Board

None.

Sheriff

None.

Superintendent of Schools

School Enumeration Record. Name of student, date of birth, etc., by school district, chronological, files, 1912-67.

Teachers' Employment Records. Information about teacher employment history, chronological, alphabetical, several books, 1912 to date.

CHOCTAW *COUNTIES*

Treasurer

None.

Cimarron (Boise City, OK 73933)

Assessor

None (no records prior to 1920).

Board of County Commissioners

None (records stored in the office of the County Clerk).

County Clerk

Surveyor's Sub-Division Records. Surveyor's description of land, handwritten, chronological, 1 book, 1910-1920.

Official Bond Book. Office held, amount of bond, and official's name, alphabetical and chronological, 1 book, 1907-1921.

Register of Claims and Claim Calendar. Chronological, 2 volumes.

Financial Ledger. Expenditures of county, record of bank balance in each account, deposits and appropriations, numerical, 5 books, 1915-1920.

Chattel Mortgage Index Record. Personal property liens, file number and date and time filed, handwritten, alphabetical, 2 books, 1907-1921.

County Deeds and Resale Deeds. Legal description, date of instrument, date and time of filing instrument, book and page, grantor and grantee, handwritten, chronological, alphabetical, indexed, 2 books, 1919-1920.

Mechanics' and Materialmens' Liens. Personal property, land description, who against, person or company filing the lien, date and time filed, alphabetical, 2 books, 1908-1921.

Commissioners' Proceedings. Minutes of commissioners' meetings, chronological, 1 volume, August 21, 1907-1920.

Physicians' Certificates. Information found on original physicians' certificates, handwritten, chronological, alphabetical, 1 book, 1908-1921.

Service Discharges. Handwritten from the original discharge, chronological and alphabetical, 1 book, 1918-1921.

Release of Mortgages. Grantor and Grantee, legal description, original mortgage filing information, date and time filed, chronological, indexed and alphabetical, 1 book, 1909-1921.

Bond Records. Description of school bonds, register of bonds and payments of interest on coupons, handwritten, chronological, 2 books, 1908-1920.

Patent Books. Grantor, grantee, land description, file stamped with date and time, amount of filing, handwritten from original, chronological, indexed and alphabetical, 6 books, 1908-1921.

Deeds Books. Grantor, grantee, land description, file stamped with date and time, amount of recording instrument, book and page, chronological, indexed and alphabetical, 20 books, 1910-1921.

Mortgage Books. Mortgagor, mortgagee, legal description, date and time filed, handwritten and typed from originals, date and number of instrument and amount, chronological, indexed and alphabetical, 11 books, 1911-1921.

Miscellaneous Books. Grantor, grantee, legal description, date and time filed, typed and handwritten, date and number of instrument, chronological, indexed and alphabetical, 8 books, 1916-1921.

General Land Office Receipts Book. Receipts given for homestead, handwritten, date of instrument, filing date, time and amount, chronological, indexed and alphabetical, 1 book, 1909-1913.

Assignment Records Book. Assignment of mortgages with name of original mortgagee and whom assigned to, legal description, time and date of filing, date of instrument and number, book and page, and amount of original mortgage, chronological, indexed and alphabetical, 1 book, 1917-1927.

Plats. Lots, sections, township and range, also have survey notes for Cimarron County, lot measurements, acreage in different sections, surveyor's note on when survey was done, chronological, alphabetical and indexed, 2 books, 1892 and 1906-1920.

Reception Record Books. Number, date and time filed, grantor, grantee, amount for recording, and to whom mailed, chronological, 4 volumes, 1907-1921.

Warrant Books. Amount of each warrant, chronological, 2 books, 1908-1921.

CIMARRON COUNTIES

Estimate of Needs. Estimate of yearly needs for budget approval, each county, city and school entity, chronological, by fiscal year, 1917-1920.

Delinquent Tax Sales. Property sold for taxes past due and not paid, chronological, 2 books, 1908-1920.

County Road System Surveys. Drafts showing county road surveys, various maps, 10 items, no date.

Tax Certificates. Certificates of delinquent taxes, chronological, numerous books, various dates.

Register Stock Brands. Registration of stock brands, chronological, 1 book, 1908-1920.

Note: Since Cimarron County was originally part of Beaver Territory, numerous land records pertaining to Cimarron County remain in Beaver County.

Court Clerk

Marriage. Chronological, index by alphabet, 7 volumes, January 8, 1908 to date.

Probate. Probate of estates, guardianships and mental health cases, include name of attorney, style number, inventories and appraisements, orders of the court, chronological, index by alphabet, 1 volume, 1908 to date.

Civil. Civil suits, divorces and small claims, include attorney names, number and style of case, judgments entered, orders of the court, chronological, index by alphabet, 1908 to date.

Criminal Appearance Docket. Name of attorneys, number and style of case, petitions, judgments, orders of the court and court costs, chronological, index by alphabet, 2 volumes, 1908 to date.

Criminal Journal. Judgment and sentence, presiding judge, chronological, no index, 1 volume, 1908 to date.

Criminal Information. County attorneys, justice of the peace, clerks of district court, witnesses, chronological, index by alphabet, 1 volume, 1908 to date.

Minister Records. Ministers registered to perform marriages in Oklahoma, chronological, index by alphabet, 1 volume, 1908 to date.

COUNTIES *CLEVELAND*

Department of Commerce and Labor, Division of Naturalization. Petition for naturalization, affidavit of witnesses, oath of allegiance, order of court, admitting petitioner, chronological, index by alphabet, 1 volume, 1908 to date.

Election Board

None.

Sheriff

Tax Warrants. Chronological, alphabetical, one book, 1908 to date.

Superintendent of Schools

Listing of County Teachers. Listing, by district, of all teachers in Cimarron County, chronological, 2 books, 1907 to date.

School District Plat Maps. Plat listings of school districts in Cimarron County, by district number, 3 volumes, 1907 to date.

Treasurer

None.

Cleveland (Norman, OK 73069)

Assessor

None (no records prior to 1921).

Board of County Commissioners

Commissioners' Proceedings. Minutes of commissioners' meetings, include details of matters discussed, actions taken, names of parties and dates, chronological, partial indexes, 5 volumes, 1890-1924.

County Clerk

Deed Book. Warranty deeds, quit claim deeds, final decree, divorce decree, mineral deeds, sheriff deeds, tax deeds, court judgments, vacation of plats, etc., chronological, also direct and reverse alphabetical index, 51 books, 1890-1920.

Mortgage Book. Mortgages, chronological, also direct and reverse alphabetical index, 15 books, 1890-1920.

CLEVELAND *COUNTIES*

Miscellaneous Book. Release of mortgage, easement, right of way, oil and gas lease, relinquishment of oil and gas lease, etc., chronological, also direct and reverse alphabetical index, 27 books, 1890-1920.

Patent Book. Patent from the United States Government, chronological and in deed, grantor-grantee (alphabetical), 4 books, 1890-1920.

Final Receipt. Final receipt (homestead), chronological and with deed - grantor and grantee index, 1 book, 1890-1920.

Federal Tax Liens. 1925-.

Discharge Records (DD-214). Discharge from service, discharge index - alphabetical, 1 book, 1890-1920.

Medical or Physician Licenses. Medical or physician licenses, alphabetical index in front of book, 1 book, 1890-1920.

Plat Book. All platted additions to Cleveland County, chronological, alphabetical index only, 1 book, 1890-1920.

Chattel Mortgage Reception Book. Daily entry of chattel mortgage filings, chronological, 1 book, 1890-1920.

Real Estate Reception Book. Daily entry of all real estate filings, deeds, mortgages, oil and gas leases, etc., chronological, 13 books, 1890-1920.

Trustee Deeds. Trustee deeds, chronological and alphabetical in grantor and grantee index.

Court Clerk

County Criminal Cases. Index, dockets and cases, alphabetical and chronological, microfilm, 1891-1920.

Marriage Records. Index and dockets, also separate listing for Lexington, alphabetical and chronological, microfilm, 1890-1920.

Civil (including Divorce). Index, dockets and cases, alphabetical and chronological, microfilm, 1891-1920.

Probate. Index, dockets and cases, alphabetical and chronological, microfilm, 1893-1920.

COUNTIES *COAL*

Election Board

    Election Record. Books containing voter registrations, precinct, name, address, date registered and age at registration, alphabetical, 1923-1956.

Sheriff

    Jail Records. All persons booked in and out of jail, name, charge, residence, description, date of discharge and date committed, chronological, 1 volume, 1907-1921.

Superintendent of Schools

    Pupils' Annual Record. Name of student, grades, attendance, etc., by school district, alphabetical, 100s of books, 1917 to date.

    Teachers' Examination Records. Information regarding issuance of teachers' county certificates, chronological, alphabetical, 18 volumes, 1902-31.

    Examination Record. Pupils' examination results, by grade, chronological, and alphabetical, 1926-59.

    School Enumeration Records (Census). Name of student, date of birth, etc., by school district, chronological, files, 1913-68.

Treasurer

    Tax Rolls (stored in courthouse attic). Lists of real estate subject to taxation, name of property owner, legal description of property, assessed value and tax dollar amount, legal description by school district, 1892-1920.

Coal (Coalgate, OK 74538)

Assessor

    Assessment Rolls. Lists all taxable property, city and town lots and blocks, and personal property for Coalgate City, total value of land and personal property, alphabetical for personal property, numerical for real property, 1 volume, 1908.

    Assessment Roll. Personal property for Phillips City, alphabetical, 1 volume, 1909.

COAL *COUNTIES*

Assessment Rolls. Lists all taxable property, city and town lots and blocks, and personal property, total value of land and personal property, alphabetical and numerical, 76 volumes, 1912-1920.

Board of County Commissioners

None.

County Clerk

Land Records. 100s of books, 1904 to date.

Dawes Commission. Land descriptions, alphabetical, 1 volume, 1907-.

Dawes Commission. Roll numbers, alphabetical, 2 volumes, 1907-.

Court Clerk

Civil. Journal entries of daily proceedings, number and style of case, judgments entered, and orders of court, chronological, index, 23 volumes, 1907 to date.

Probate. Journal entries of daily proceedings, number and style of case, judgments entered, and orders of court, chronological, index, 6 volumes, 1907 to date.

Small Claims. Journal entries of daily proceedings, number and style of case, judgments entered, and orders of court, chronological, index, 3 volumes, 1969 to date.

Divorce. Journal entries of daily proceedings, number and style of case, judgments entered, and orders of court, chronological, index, 4 volumes, 1966 to date.

Guardianship. Journal entries of daily proceedings, number and style of case, judgments entered, and orders of court, chronological, index, 5 volumes, 1907 to date.

Marriages. Application, marriage record, chronological, index, 16 volumes, 1907 to date.

Traffic. Journal entries of daily proceedings, number and style of case, judgments entered, and orders of court, chronological, index, 9 volumes, 1969 to date.

Felony. Journal entries of daily proceedings, number and style of case, judgments entered, and orders of court, chronological, index, 2 books, 1980 to date.

Criminal/Felony. Journal entries of daily proceedings, number and style of case, judgments entered, and orders of court, chronological, index, volumes 1-19 (criminal), volumes 1-2 (felony), 1907 to date.

Election Board

None.

Historical and Mining Museum, Coal County, Coalgate, Oklahoma

Commissioners' Journal. 2 volumes, 1908-1911 and 1917-1920.

Trial Docket. Criminal, 8 volumes, 1908-1913 and 1916-1920.

Justice of the Peace Docket. Criminal, 21 volumes, 1908-1921.

Trial Docket. Civil, 5 volumes, 1908-1913 and 1918-1921.

Justice of the Peace Docket. Civil, 6 volumes, 1908-1910 and 1913-1920.

Collection Register. 3 volumes, 1918-1924.

Claim and Warrant Register. 5 volumes, 1909 to date and 1916-1943.

Mortgage Record. 1 volume, no date.

Journal. Civil, 2 volumes, 1913-1938.

Attorneys' Receipt for Papers. 2 volumes, 1908-1918.

List of Delinquent Taxes. 6 volumes, 1909-1942.

Assessment Rolls. 33 volumes, 1908-1911 and 1917-1918.

Tax Receipts. 16 volumes, 1910.

Cash Record - Water. 2 volumes, 1910-1914.

Investment Record. 1 volume, 1914 to date.

Record of Indictments. 1 volume, 1909-1911.

Record of Bridges Erected and Repaired. 1 volume, 1909-1911.

Widows' Pension Record. 1 volume, 1916-1925.

Journal - Criminal. 1 volume, 1911-1913.

Register Certificate of Error. 1 volume, 1916.

Guardians' Report Record. 1 volume, 1908-1911.

Township Ledger. 1 volume, 1914-1927.

Treasurer's Daily Report. 1 volume, 1911.

Township Warrant Register. 1 volume, 1914-1916.

Fee Book. 1 volume, 1907-1922.

Depository Bond Record. 1 volume, 1919-1925.

Treasurer's Depository Register. 1 volume, 1917-1922.

Attorneys' Receipts for Papers. 1 volume, 1919-1923.

School Fund Ledger. 2 volumes, 1908-09 and 1917-1919.

Minute Book - District Court. 2 volumes, 1900-1916.

Examining Magistrate Record. 1 volume, 1920-1936.

Town Lot Record. 1 volume. 1913.

Land List. 1 volume, no date.

Back Tax Record. 1 volume, 1919-1920.

Cash Book - County Court. 3 volumes, 1910-1923.

Jury Record - District Court. 1 volume, 1908-1918.

Probate Bench Docket - County Court. 1 volume, 1908-1916.

Inheritance Tax Record - County Court. 1 volume, 1911-1920.

Sheriffs' Receipts for Tax Warrants. 1 volume, 1908-1933.

COUNTIES   COAL

Delinquent Tax Sale Record. 1 volume, 1909-1917.

Motion Docket. 1 volume, 1909-1945.

School District Sinking Fund. 1 volume, 1918-1921.

Foreign Fee Record. 1 volume, 192?

Information Record. 1 volume, 1908-

Payment Register. 1 volume, 1915-1917.

Collection and Distribution Record. 5 volumes, 1910-1945.

Sheriffs' Record - Criminal. 3 volumes, 1913-1934.

Certificate of Assessment. 1 volume, 1916-1917.

Calendar Docket. 1 volume, 1911.

Assessment List. 1 volume, 1917.

Tax Book - City Clerk's Office. 1 volume, 1916-1917.

Register of Bonds. 1 volume, 1906-1946.

Journal - Water. 1 volume, 1911-1914.

Sinking Fund Investments. 1 volume, 1910-1935.

Ledger - Coalgate Treasurer. 1 volume, 1909-1913.

Personal Tax Roll. 1 volume, 1907-1908.

Civil Process Record - Sheriff. 1 volume, 1920-1924.

Criminal Process Record - Sheriff. 1 volume, 1919-1927.

Tax Warrant Record - Sheriff. 1 volume, 1911-1917.

Tax Fee Record - Sheriff. 1 volume, 1911-1913.

Coalgate City Schools' Enrollment. 1 volume, 1909-1913.

Marriage Book. 1 volume, 1907-1908.

COAL *COUNTIES*

Choctaw Nation Marriage Records. 3 volumes, 1890-1894 and 1907-1910.

Indian Territory Marriage Records (Atoka County). 1 volume, 1897-1899.

Marriage Records. 1 volume, 1908-1923.

Cemetery Records. Coalgate, Hearrell, Cairo, Davis, Moore, Centrahoma, Lehigh, Boggy Depot, Globe, Nixon, Wilson, and Woodmen of the World, quantity unknown, no date.

Sheriff

None.

Superintendent of Schools

School Enumeration Record (Census). Name of student, age, academic records, chronological and alphabetical, 100s of books, 1909 to date.

Treasurer

Tax Rolls. Chronological, alphabetical, 80 books, 1910-1920.

Comanche (Lawton, OK 73501)

Assessor

None.

Board of County Commissioners

None (records prior to 1921 stored in the office of the County Clerk).

County Clerk

Mortgage. Copies of mortgages on real property, date, book and page of recording, names of mortgagor and mortgagee, amount of mortgage, legal description, date of instrument, 60 volumes, 1901-1921.

Deed. Copies of deeds, date, book and page of recording, names of grantor and grantee, legal description, date of instrument, 74 volumes, 1901-1921.

Oil and Gas Lease. Copies of lease, date, book and page of recording, names of lessor and lessee, legal description, date of instrument, 6 volumes, 1901-1921.

Administrative Record. Petition for letters of administration and order for hearing on petition, date, book and page of recording, deceased person's name, legal description of property, date of instrument, 2 volumes, 1901-1921.

Townsite Certificate. Copies of certificate, date, book and page of recording, description of property, date of instrument, 1 volume, 1901-1921.

Release and Assignment. Copies of release and assignment, grantor, grantee, date, book and page of recording, description of property, date of instrument, 11 volumes, 1901-1921.

Certificate of Purchase Record. Copies of instrument, date, book and page of recording, legal description, date of instrument, 1 volume, 1901-1921.

Quit Claim Deed Record. Copy of deed, grantor, grantee, date, book and page of recording, legal description, date of instrument, 2 volumes, 1901-1921.

Resale Deed Record. Copy of deed, grantee, date, book and page of recording, legal description, date of instrument, 1 volume, 1901-1921.

Release Record. Grantor, grantee, copy of release, date, book and page of recording, date of instrument, 6 volumes, 1901-1921.

Tax Deed. Copy of deed, grantee, date, book and page of recording, description of property, date of instrument, 1 volume, 1901-1921.

Receivers Receipt Record. Date, book and page of recording, copy of instrument, date of instrument, grantee, 1 volume, 1901-1921.

Miscellaneous Record. Copies of instrument, date, book and page of recording, grantor, grantee, legal description, date of instrument, 13 volumes, 1901-1921.

Patent. Copies of instrument, date, book and page of recording, grantee, legal description, date of instrument, 7 volumes, 1901-1921.

Homestead Receipt. Copies of receipt, date, book and page of recording, grantee, legal description, date of instrument, 1 volume, 1901-1921.

Mineral Location Record. Copies of instrument, date, book and page of recording, location, claimant, date of claim, 1 volume, 1901-1921.

COMANCHE *COUNTIES*

Receipt and Patent. Grantor, grantee, date of instrument, copy of instrument, date, book and page of recording, legal description, 1 volume, 1901-1921.

Final Receipt. Copy of instrument, date, book and page of recording, description, grantee, date of instrument, 1 volume, 1901-1921.

Grantor. Grantor, grantee, date of recording, date of instrument, brief description, book and page, 3 volumes, 1901-1921.

Grantee. Grantee, grantor, date of recording, date of instrument, brief description, book and page, 3 volumes, 1901-1921.

Mortgagor. Mortgagor, mortgagee, date of recording, date of instrument, brief description, book and page, 3 volumes, 1901-1921.

Miscellaneous. Grantor, grantee, date of recording, date of instrument, brief description, book and page, 2 volumes, 1901-1921.

Commissioners' Proceedings. Minutes of meetings of county commissioners, date of meeting, action taken, 4 volumes, 1901-1921.

Mortgagee. Mortgagee, mortgagor, date of recording, date of instrument, brief description, book and page, 3 volumes, 1901-1921.

Note: Security copies of all records stored in mine.

Court Clerk

Probate. Index, docket and cases, chronological, 28 volumes, 1901 to date.

Felony. Index, docket and cases, chronological, 39 volumes, 1901 to date.

Marriage License. Index, docket and cases, chronological, 135 volumes, 1901 to date.

Civil. Index, docket and cases, chronological, 90 volumes, 1901 to date.

Divorce. Index, docket and cases, chronological, 57 volumes, 1901 to date.

Adoption. Index, docket and cases, chronological, 4 volumes, 1901 to date.

Small Claims. Index, docket and cases, chronological, 40 volumes, 1969 to date.

Beer License. Index, docket and cases, chronological, 20 volumes.

Juvenile. Index, docket and cases, 11 volumes.

Mental Health. Index, docket and cases, chronological, 3 volumes.

Notary. Index and docket, chronological, 26 volumes.

Ministers' Credentials. Index, chronological, 2 volumes.

Misdemeanor. Index, docket and cases, chronological, 28 volumes, 1901 to date.

Traffic. Index, docket and cases, chronological, 69 volumes, 1901 to date.

Note: Additional records stored in the Museum of the Great Plains, Lawton, OK.

Election Board

None.

Lawton Public Library, Lawton, OK

Highland Cemetery, Lawton, OK. Owners of plots, index to burials by plot, chronological, alphabetical, 1 roll film, 1 notebook (pencil copy), 1901-ca. 1978.

School Census of Comanche County, Oklahoma. Microfilm of census cards in the county superintendent's office, name of student, date of birth, etc., alphabetical, 7 rolls, 1918-1968.

Oklahoma Tract Books, Bureau of Land Management, Eastern States Office (microfilm). Land ownership of Oklahoma, including Indians' allotments, and homesteads, names of persons, place owned, certificate numbers, by legal description, rolls 1-22 of Volumes 1-72, 1889-1937.

Lawton, Oklahoma Music Club (microfilm). Memberships, meetings and newspaper clippings concerning members and club activities, chronological, 3 rolls, 1901-1958.

Marriage Records, Custer County, Oklahoma Territory and Oklahoma (microfilm). Index to grooms, marriage applications and certificates, chronological, 18 rolls, 1894-1978.

Marriage Records, Beckham County, Oklahoma (microfilm). Index to grooms, marriage applications and certificates, names of bride and groom, witnesses, sometimes parents or other relatives and officiate, chronological, 19 rolls of 35 volumes, 1910-1970.

Marriage Records, Greer County, Oklahoma (microfilm). Index to grooms, marriage applications and certificates, alphabetical and chronological, 24 rolls, 1907-1977.

Tax Rolls, Greer County, Oklahoma (microfilm). Legal description of land, registered value, amount of state and school tax, by whom paid or to whom paid, real and personal property, alphabetical, 20 rolls, 1896-1926.

Marriage Rolls, Harmon County, Oklahoma (microfilm). Licenses, names of bride, groom, witnesses, sometimes parents, and officiate, alphabetical by grooms, then applications chronological, 9 rolls, 1901-1974.

Marriage Rolls, Roger Mills County, Oklahoma (microfilm). Index to grooms, etc., mostly chronological, 10 rolls, 1893-1979.

Court Records, Roger Mills County, Oklahoma (microfilm). Court journal, criminal appearance docket, journal for County F, probate and tax rolls, chronological, 37 rolls, 1896-1924.

Declaration of Intention, Roger Mills County, Oklahoma (microfilm). Declaration of intention, guardian records, town site records, civil appearance docket, chronological, 10 rolls, 1896-1924.

Oklahoma Documents (microfiche). Chronological, 4 drawers.

Index to 1911 Tax Lists of Comanche County, Oklahoma. Keyed to 1910 federal census of Comanche County compiled by Jewell R. Tankersley, maps, gives number of microfilm roll for a given township in Comanche County, by township and alphabetical, 1 book, 1910-1911.

Greer County, Oklahoma, Bloomington Precinct. Voter registrations, by registration, index at end of booklet, 1 volume, 1935.

Township Maps of Southwestern Oklahoma. Keyed to 1910 federal census rolls by township, alphabetical by county, 1 book, 1910.

Kiowa Indian Mission. Indian children and mission schools they attended, gives age and year attended, some white children, matron, and teachers, compiled by Helen Diester Bolt, loosely alphabetized by mission, full name index, 1 volume, 1881-1914.

COUNTIES *COMANCHE*

Cemeteries on Fort Sill, Oklahoma. Transcribed from tombstones and from cemetery record book, main post and County F Indian cemeteries, full index of all persons mentioned, by section then grave, 1 volume, 1869-1978.

Ootipoby Comanche Indian Cemetery. Cemetery history, list of persons buried there, history of individuals and families, Comanche Indian history and stories, bibliography, full name index, by section then grave, 1 volume, 1888-1988.

Owners of Cattle Brands Recorded at Old Red Store, Oklahoma Territory. Brands reproduced, owner, address, where herds ran, also owners of brands in west Texas, with ear marks and brands, as recorded, full name index, 1 volume, 1891-1942.

Note: The following records are stored in the Comanche County Courthouse.

Deeds, Estate Settlements and Probates. Grantor, grantee indexes to landowners, indexes, then chronological, 1898 to date.

Guardianships. Court decisions, index, then chronological, 1907 to date.

Veterans' Records of Spanish - American War and World War I. Name, rank, where served, how long, service given, sometimes home address, awards, approximately 6 volumes, 1898-1918.

Marriages. Marriages in Comanche County, index, then chronological, volumes and on microfilm, 1901 to date.

Doctors, Dentists, Lawyers, etc. Miscellaneous records, etc., incomplete, chronological, 1901-.

Museum of the Great Plains, Lawton, OK

Court Clerk Records. Civil, criminal, probate, superior court, district court, chronological, no index, 250 linear feet, 1901-1920.

Municipal Warrant Register. Warrants issued, treasurers' warrant register, warrant register, city warrants, salary fund, collection and distribution warrant register, chronological, 5 boxes, 1906-1920.

Treasurers' Reports and Registers. Monthly report, settlement report, and register of treasurer, chronological, 5 boxes, 1905-1920.

Council Meetings. Roll call, newspaper clippings, chronological, 1 box, 1904-1907.

Bond Register. City improvements, funding bonds, street improvements, storm sewers, water works, paving bonds by block and lot number, chronological, 1 box, 1903-1911 and 1917-1920.

Street Improvement Register. Chronological, 1 box, 1908-1920.

Cash Book. Individual cash account collection, chronological (gives street location), 1 box, 1904-1906 and 1910-1913.

Collection and Distribution Record. Chronological, 1 box, 1918-1920.

Claim Register and Fund Register. Chronological, 2 boxes, 1905-1920.

Voter Registration Book. General, and wards 1, 3, 4, and 5 specific, 1 box, 1906-1908.

Commissioners' Proceedings. Includes list of property owners and locations, chronological, 2 boxes, 1901-1910.

Justice Docket. Chronological, 1 box, 1903-1904.

Police Docket. Chronological, 1 box, 1904-1905.

Ordinance Record. Chronological, 1 box, 1901-1909.

Occupation License Register. Chronological, 1 box, 1912-1920.

General Ledger. Daily balance, pamphlet of city charter, chronological, 1 box, 1911.

Assessment and Tax Roll. Chronological, 1 box, 1909-1920.

List of Township Description and Assessment of Tax. Complete list of lots sold with amount paid, lot number and purchaser, newspaper clippings attached to monthly reports of city, chronological, 1 box, 1902-1918.

Sheriff

None.

Superintendent of Schools

School District Records. School district records, information concerning consolidations, chronological, 2 ledgers, 1902-1950s.

Teacher Records. Includes name, age, salary, school district, etc., chronological, alphabetical, 1 ledger, 1903-1940s.

Census Record of School Enrollments. Includes date of birth, age, parents' name, area of school, etc., chronological, alphabetical, 20 linear feet, 1918-1967.

Treasurer

Tax Rolls. None prior to 1921.

Cotton (Walters, OK 73572)

Assessor

None.

Board of County Commissioners

Records stored in the office of the County Clerk.

County Clerk

Land Records. Deeds, mortgages, patents, oil and gas leases, release of mortgages, release of oil and gas leases, etc., chronological, 238 volumes, 1902 to date.

Grantor/Grantee Index of Land Records. Grantor/grantee and reverse index, alphabetical and type of entry (mortgage, deed or miscellaneous), 16 volumes, 1902 to date.

County Commissioners' Minutes. Minutes of board meetings, chronological, 10 volumes, 1912 to date.

County Register of Electors. List of voters, by precinct and chronological, 2 volumes, 1916-1952.

Physician Register. Register of physician and medical degree, chronological, 1 volume, 1912 to date.

Surveyor Notes - Field Notes. Kiowa, Comanche and Apache lands lying south of 35th parallel of north latitude, also leased lands south of north fork of Red River in the Indian Territory, by location, 2 volumes, 1873-1874.

COTTON   COUNTIES

    Government Survey Plat. Plat showing survey - metes, bounds, number of acres, etc., 1 volume, 1874.

    School Records. All records that would normally be kept by the county superintendent of schools, by school district and chronological, 4 file cabinets, 1913-1965.

    Birth Records. Original birth certificates, chronological and alphabetical, 2 file drawers, 1917-1952.

    Death Records. Original death certificates, chronological and alphabetical, 2 file drawers, 1918-57.

    Census Enumeration. 100-150 books, 1918-1968.

Court Clerk

    Probate. Index, dockets and cases, chronological, index - alphabetical, 1 book, 1912-1920.

    Civil. Index, dockets and cases, includes divorce, chronological, 4 books, 1912-1920.

    Marriage Licenses. Index and dockets, alphabetical and chronological, 2 books, 1912-20.

    Criminal. Index and dockets, chronological, 2 books, 1912-1920.

Election Board

    Election Records. None prior to 1920.

Sheriff

    None.

Superintendent of Schools

    Records stored in the office of the County Clerk.

Treasurer

    No tax records prior to 1921.

COUNTIES   CRAIG

Craig (Vinita, OK 74301)

Assessor

   Assessment Rolls. Record of all taxable property in county, location and value, by township, section and range, 300 volumes, 1939 to date.

Board of County Commissioners

   Records stored in the office of the County Clerk.

County Clerk

   Land Records. Index, land tract, chronological and alphabetical, 1907 to date.

Court Clerk

   Civil Cases. Number and style of case, names of attorneys, judgments entered, orders of court, docket sheets, entire case file, chronological, alphabetical cross index, 6 dockets, November 21, 1907-1921.

   Divorce Cases. Number and style of case, names of attorneys, judgments entered, orders of court, docket sheets, entire case file, chronological, alphabetical cross index, 6 dockets, November 21, 1907-1921.

   Probate Cases. Number and style of case, names of attorneys, judgments entered, orders of court, docket sheets, entire case file, chronological, alphabetical cross index, 6 dockets, November 1907-1921.

   Criminal Cases - Felonies. Number and style of case, names of attorneys, judgments entered, orders of court, docket sheets, entire case file, chronological, alphabetical cross index, 2 dockets, November 11, 1907-1921.

   Marriage Records. Application and marriage license, date of application, date and location of marriage, alphabetical, chronological, 13 dockets, 1902-1921.

   Note: Vinita Public Library, Vinita, OK has some civil, divorce and marriage records (no criminal).

Election Board

   Elections. None prior to 1921.

   Filings. None prior to 1921.

CRAIG *COUNTIES*

Public Library, Vinita, Oklahoma

>Probate Records - Northern District of Cherokee Nation. 4 volumes, 1884-1914.
>
>Cherokee Nation Records. Permits, marriages, wills and estates, microfilm, 1858-1898.
>
>Indian Territory Marriage Records. Microfilm, 1902-1907.
>
>Civil Court Files. Divorce, marriage, etc., 80 rolls, 1904- .
>
>Cherokee Nation Records. Permits, marriages, wills and estates, microfilm, 1858-1898.
>
>Oklahoma Marriage Record Books, Craig County. Microfilm, 1909-1936.
>
>Probate Files, Craig County. Microfilm, 1892-1908.

Sheriff

>None.

Superintendent of Schools

>School Census. Dates of birth of school age children, chronological and by school number, 1912 and 1922-1969.
>
>Dependent School Registers. Student transcripts, chronological, 1930-1959.
>
>School Plats. Where school is located in county, numerical, 1909 to date.
>
>Annexation and Consolidation of County Schools. Numerical, 1909 to date.
>
>Dependent School Teachers' Contracts. Yearly contracts between teacher and school board, numerical and chronological, 1909 to date.
>
>Report of School Board Clerks to County Superintendent. Proceedings of school board business, numerical and chronological, 1909-1959.
>
>Note: Additional records stored in the Vinita Public Library, Vinita, OK.

Treasurer

>Original 1908 Tax Rolls (stored in the Vinita Public Library, Vinita, OK). By name and property description, 1908.

COUNTIES *CREEK*

Creek (Sapulpa, OK 74066)

Assessor

　　None.

Board of County Commissioners

　　None (Commissioners' Journals stored in the office of the County Clerk).

County Clerk

　　Deed Records, Grantor-Grantee. Names of grantors and grantees, date of instrument and recording date, book and page where recorded, exact information can be obtained by checking recorded document, chronological, indexed alphabetical and posted to tract indexes, ca. 1900-1920.

　　Mortgage Records, Grantor-Grantee. Names of mortgagors and mortgagees, date of instrument and recording date, book and page where recorded, exact information can be obtained by checking recorded document, chronological, indexed alphabetical and posted to tract indexes, ca. 1900-1920.

　　Miscellaneous Records, Grantor-Grantee. Names of grantors and grantees, types of instruments recorded, date and recording date, book and page where recorded, exact information can be obtained by checking recorded document, chronological, indexed alphabetical and posted to tract indexes, ca. 1900-1920.

　　Partial Grantor-Grantee Allotment and Homestead Deeds. Roll number, name of allottee (Creek Indian), date of deed, recording information and legal description (record incomplete because all deeds were not recorded at time received), chronological, alphabetical, 1 volume, ca. 1898-1920.

　　Land Records, Indian Territory. By legal description and chronological, no alphabetical indexes, volumes "A" - "W", approximately 1898-1907.

　　Land Records, Indian Territory. By legal description and chronological, no alphabetical indexes, volumes 1-33, approximately 1898-1907.

　　Townsite Records. Filings of townsite patents to the four patented towns in Creek County by the Department of the Interior, chronological, 1 book, ca. 1904-1908.

　　Patent Records. Filings of homestead deeds and allotment deeds to tract lands from the Department of the Interior, Muskogee, Creek Nation, chronological, 5 books, prior to 1907.

CREEK *COUNTIES*

Miscellaneous Transcribed Records from Okmulgee County. Varied documents recorded in Okmulgee County, no alphabetical index, posted on tract indexes, 6 books, prior to 1907.

Oil and Gas Lease Records. Transcribed oil and gas lease records from the Department of the Interior, Indian Territory, no alphabetical index, indexed by tract only, 2 books, prior to 1907.

Commissioners' Journals. Minutes of commissioners' meetings and lists of warrants paid, book 1 missing from office for many years, chronological, 4 books, April 3, 1911-1920.

Servicemens' Discharge Records. World War I and possibly a few Spanish American War discharges, alphabetical, 2 books plus recordings scattered through other books, 1898- ca. 1920.

Court Clerk

Probate. Docket and cases, numerical, 1 volume and microfilm, 1907-1921.

Superior Court (Civil and Domestic Relations). Docket and cases, numerical, 17 volumes and microfilm, 1917-1921.

Judgment Docket. Docket, chronological, 3 volumes, 1908-1921.

Criminal. Docket, index and cases, numerical, 2 volumes, 1904-1921.

Marriage License. Index and license, chronological, 13 volumes, 1907-1921.

Lunacy (Mental Health). Index, dockets and cases, numerical, 3 volumes, 1907-1921.

Note: Additional records stored in the Oklahoma Department of Libraries, Oklahoma City, OK.

Election Board

None.

Sheriff

None.

COUNTIES *CUSTER*

Superintendent of Schools

> School Enumeration Record (Census). Name of student, date of birth, etc., by school district, chronological, 500-600 books, also microfilm, 1917-1968.
>
> Retirement Records. Early-day teachers.

Treasurer

> None.

Custer (Arapaho, OK 73620)

Assessor

> None.

Board of County Commissioners

> Commissioners' Journals. Minutes of proceedings, includes details of matters discussed, actions taken, names of parties, and all dates, chronological, no index, 7 volumes, 1896-1920.

County Clerk

> Real Estate. Copies of original documents such as patents, judgments, dockets, etc., chronological and alphabetical, 867 volumes, 1896 to date.
>
> Uniform Commercial Code, Financing Statements. Filings pertaining to Uniform Commercial Code, file cards, alphabetical, 1977 to date.

Court Clerk

> Marriage Licenses. Chronological, alphabetical, 2-3 books, 1895-1920.
>
> Civil Cases. Includes divorces, chronological, alphabetical, 10-15 books, 1896-1920.
>
> Probate Record. Adoption, guardianship and probate, chronological, 2 books, 1900-20.

Election Board

> None (earliest records date back to 1930s).

CUSTER *COUNTIES*

Sheriff

>Jail Log County G. All arrests, dates, names, charges, descriptions, chronological, 1 volume, 1895 to date.

Superintendent of Schools

>Records stored in the office of the County Clerk.

Treasurer

>None.

Delaware (Jay, OK 74346)

Assessor

>Land Indexing Book. On computer as of 1988, chronological, 294 volumes, 1940 to date.

Board of County Commissioners

>Minutes of Meetings. Chronological, 8 journals, 1940 to date.

County Clerk

>Land Index. Original documents and computerized data, by legal description, 66 volumes (legal description), 581 original documents, and on computer since 1987, 1905 to date.

Court Clerk

>Cases, Civil. Alphabetical, 29 volumes, 1911 to date.

>Cases, Probate. Alphabetical, 11 volumes, 1911 to date.

>Cases, Misdemeanor. Alphabetical, 16 volumes, 1911 to date.

Election Board

>None.

Sheriff
>None.

COUNTIES *DEWEY*

Superintendent of Schools

Scholastic Reports and Payroll Salary Reports. Alphabetical, 1889-.

Treasurer

Ad Valorem Taxes. Collection of ad valorem taxes, distribution to schools and entities, alphabetical, 6,000 parcels, 1916 to date.

Dewey (Taloga, OK 73667)

Assessor

Records stored in old building behind courthouse (inaccessible).

Board of County Commissioners

Commissioners' Proceedings. Minutes of commissioners' meetings, chronological, 4 volumes, 1892-1921.

County Clerk

Final Receipt. Chronological, 2 books, 1892-1905.

Patent. Chronological, 5 books, 1901-1921.

Deeds. Chronological, 25 books, 1892-1921.

Miscellaneous Records. Chronological, 13 books, 1892-1921.

Honorable Discharge. Alphabetical, 1 book, 1919-1921.

Court Clerk

Letters Testamentary. Chronological, 1 volume, 1901-1919.

Miscellaneous Records. 1 volume, 1908-1914.

Order Book. 1 volume, 1895-1909.

Execution Docket. Record of orders carried out by sheriff's department, chronological, 1 volume, 1896-1916.

Mechanics' Lien Record. Chronological, 1 volume, 1894-1960.

Judgment Docket. Alphabetical, 1 volume, 1895-1913.

Probate Records. Wills and estates, chronological, 2 volumes, 1902-1926.

Marriage Records. Contains marriage licenses, chronological, 5 volumes, 1895-1925.

Civil. Divorce and lawsuit records, chronological, 2 volumes, 1911-1924.

Court Journal. Record of cases, chronological, 4 volumes, 1904-1924.

Lunacy Record. People committed to state hospitals, chronological, 1 volume, 1917-1942.

Inventory and Appraisement of Estates. Chronological, 3 volumes, 1901-1929.

Criminal Docket. Record of lawsuits, chronological, 1 volume, 1891-1922.

Guardians' Report. Chronological, 1 volume, 1902-1922.

Will Record. Will and testimony in probate, chronological, 1 volume, 1901-1913.

Election Board

None.

Sheriff

Sheriffs' Record. Process service, arrests made, chronological, alphabetical, 1 ledger, June 11, 1895 to date.

Superintendent of Schools

School Records. Listing of family members by school districts, chronological, approximately 85 books for each year, 1912-1921.

Treasurer

None.

COUNTIES *ELLIS*

Ellis (Arnett, OK 73832)

Assessor

> Record of School District Officers, Day County. Names, addresses, school district numbers, dates, chronological, 1 volume, 1893-1907.
>
> School District Boundaries, Day County. Maps, numerical, 1 volume, 1893-1907.
>
> Normal Institute, Day County. Names of applicants, graduates, test scores, fees, chronological, 2 volumes, 1893-1907.
>
> Day County Daily Record. Superintendent's diary, July 1901 to October 1902, enrollment rolls (names and ages), superintendent's itinerary, 1 volume, 1901-1902.
>
> Records of Day County Superintendent. Diary, enrollment rolls for all districts, chronological, 1 volume, 1894-1901.

Board of County Commissioners

> Commissioners' Proceedings. Chronological, 8 volumes, 1898 to date.

County Clerk

> Mortgages. Exact copies of mortgages on property, date, names of mortgagor and mortgagee, amount, legal description of property, date and time filed, chronological, indexed alphabetical, 33 volumes, 1901-1920.
>
> Deeds. Exact copies of deeds on property, date, names of grantor and grantee, legal description of property, date and time filed, chronological, indexed alphabetical, 25 volumes, 1896-1920.
>
> Patents. Legal description of property, date and time filed, names of landholders, date of instrument, indexed alphabetical, commuted copies from before statehood and formation of Ellis County, 9 volumes, 1900-1920.
>
> Final Receipts. Commuted copies, land description, date filed, date of instrument, chronological, indexed alphabetical, 5 volumes, 1900-1922.
>
> Miscellaneous. Exact copies, date, names of grantor and grantee, legal description of property, date and time filed, chronological, indexed alphabetical, 13 volumes, 1897-1920.

Mortgage Releases. Exact copies of mortgage releases on real property, date of instrument, names of mortgagor and mortgagee, date releases, legal description, date and time filed, chronological, indexed alphabetical, 7 volumes, 1908-1920.

Court Clerk

Probate. Index, dockets and cases, chronological and alphabetical, 3 volumes, 1901-1920.

Civil. Index, dockets and cases, chronological and alphabetical, 8 volumes, 1907-1920.

Marriage. Index, docket and some original licenses, chronological and alphabetical, 4 volumes, 1892-1920.

Felony. Index, docket and cases, chronological and alphabetical, 1 volume, 1907-1920.

Election Board

Old Registration Books (random, not a complete set). Voter registrations in "old-time" precincts, include registration dates, names, and birth dates, arranged by precincts, 32 volumes, 1916-1958.

Brand Book. Names and drawings of cattle brands showing where located on cow, 1 volume, no dates.

Receipt Book. Payments for services in elections, 1 volume, 1920-1921.

Note: There are few records with early dates because many records were destroyed by termites.

Sheriff

None.

Superintendent of Schools

Records stored in the office of the Assessor.

Treasurer

Tax Rolls. Taxpayer (owner of property), description, location and value of property, amount of tax, by legal description, 1910-1920.

COUNTIES   *GARFIELD*

Resale Record. Description of property, who bought property, amount paid for property at resale, chronological, 2 volumes, 1902-1920.

Delinquent Tax Sale. Description, purchaser, amount sold for, by legal description, 1 volume, 1902-1906.

Treasurers' Distribution Record. Accounts of tax money, to whom distributed, 1897-?.

Note: These records have limited access, thus it is difficult to provide an accurate accounting.

Garfield (Enid, OK 73701)

Assessor

All records prior to 1982 are stored in the Garfield County Historical Society, Enid, OK.

Board of County Commissioners

Commissioners' Journal. Minutes of proceedings, includes details of matters discussed, actions taken, names of parties, and all dates, chronological, 5 volumes, November 4, 1893 to December 17, 1927, except January 4, 1897 through July 1, 1901 (lost in courthouse fire).

County Clerk

Deed Records. Exact copies of deeds on real property, date and instrument number and filing date, names of the buyers and sellers, documentary stamp, legal description of property, time filed, indexed chronologically, 102 volumes, 1893-1920.

Mortgage Records. Exact copies of mortgages on real property, date and instrument number and filing date and time, names of mortgagor and mortgagee, legal description of property, and amount and conditions of loan, indexed chronologically, 92 volumes, 1893-1920.

Miscellaneous Records. Exact copies of instruments dealing with oil and gas leases, minerals, easements, agreements, leases, probates, etc., date and instrument number and filing date and time, legal descriptions, names of grantor and grantee, indexed chronologically, 22 volumes, 1898-1920.

Patent and Final Receipt Records. Exact copies of patent and final receipts on real property, date and instrument number and filing date and time, legal description, names of grantor and grantee, indexed chronologically, 8 volumes, 1895-1913.

Grantor/Grantee Records. Names of grantor and grantee, filing date and time, legal description, type of instrument, indexed alphabetically, 9 volumes, 1893-1920.

Plat Records. Original plat records on real property, date and number of plat and time filed, dimension of lots, shows the building lines, utility easements, rights of way, etc., indexed chronologically, 1894 to date.

Court Clerk

Probate. Index, dockets and cases, chronological, 1893-1920.

Marriage. Index, applications and certificates, chronological, 1893-1920.

Divorce. Index, filmed cases, chronological, 1893-1920.

Civil. Index, filmed cases, chronological, 1893-1920.

Election Board

Election Record. Date of election, number of votes cast for each candidate in each precinct, total votes cast for all candidates, and minutes, chronological, 1 volume, 1908-1920.

Museum of the Cherokee Strip, Enid, OK

Delinquent Personal Tax Roll. Name of person assessed, tax for what year, where assessed, number of school district, final assessed valuation, territorial tax, county, township and municipal tax, school tax, receipt number, etc., 1 volume, 1894-1904.

Tax Roll. Legal description, number of acres, number of school district, valuation, territorial tax, county general, county school, county board interest, county sinking fund, city and township tax, township road and bridge, etc., 10 volumes, 1894-1909.

Tax Roll - Lots. Legal description, number of acres, school district, assessed value, county equalized value, taxes, payments, receipts, rebate, cost advertising, date of sale, etc., 9 volumes, 1905-1909.

COUNTIES *GARVIN*

Tax Roll - Real Estate. Section lot, township, range/block, number of school district, total assessed value, taxes, payments, number of receipts, payments, penalty, list and certain fees, cost and penalties, date of sale, etc., 7 volumes, 1895-1906.

Tax Roll - Personal and Real. Legal description, number of acres, school district, assessed value, consolidated territorial taxes, taxes, payments, number of receipt, payment, rebate, fees, date of sale, certificate number, etc., 11 volumes, 1895-1906.

Sheriff

None.

Superintendent of Schools

Early records stored in the office of the County Clerk.

Treasurer

Records stored in the Museum of the Cherokee Strip, Enid, OK.

Garvin (Pauls Valley, OK 73075)

Assessor

None (records kept for 10 years).

Board of County Commissioners

None.

County Clerk

Miscellaneous Records. Chronological, 1,253 books, January 18, 1903 to date.

Warranty Deed Records. Chronological, 67 books, January 3, 1906 to June 25, 1951.

Mineral Deed Records. Chronological, 21 books, April 23, 1942 to August 29, 1951.

Patent Records (Allotments). Chronological, 4 volumes, July 30, 1903 to July 28, 1905.

Honorable Discharge Records. Chronological, 12 books, March 22, 1919 to date.

Court Clerk

Probate, Civil, Criminal, Marriage, Adoption, Small Claims and Divorce Records. 1907 to date.

Note: For records prior to 1907, consult office of the Court Clerk, Ardmore, OK.

Election Board

None (no records prior to 1921).

Sheriff

None.

Superintendent of Schools

School Enumeration Record (Census). Name of student, date of birth, etc., by school district, chronological, 100s of books, 1912-1965.

Teacher Employment Record. Chronological, alphabetical, approximately 30 books, 1919 to date.

Graduation Registers - Eighth Grade. Names of students, grades, attendance, etc., chronological, alphabetical, 3-4 books, ca. 1918 to date.

Enrollment Cards. Chronological, alphabetical, ca. 1912 to date.

School District Boundary Survey. By legal description, 1 book, no date.

Treasurer

Tax Rolls. Lists of real and personal property subject to taxation, shows name and address of property owner, description of property, number of school district located, state equalized value, etc., by legal description, 6 volumes per year, 1955 to date.

Apportionment. Revenue apportioned to schools, 1 volume, 1918.

Daily Report Book. 1968 to date.

COUNTIES *GRADY*

Official Depository Ledger. 1964 to date.

Official Depository Register. 1957 to date.

Payment Register. 1915 to date.

Grady (Chickasha, OK 73018)

Assessor

Assessment Rolls. Lists of all lands in county, lots and blocks in towns and cities, personal property, chronological and legal description, 64 volumes, 1915-1920.

Board of County Commissioners

None.

County Clerk

Record Books. Copies of original documents, chronological, 172 volumes, 1903-1920.

Tract Indexes. Grantor/grantee, type of instrument, legal description of property, book and page where copy is on file, chronological, 24 volumes, 1903-1920.

Deed Index. Grantor/grantee, type of instrument, book and page where copy is on file, date of instrument and recording, brief legal description, alphabetical, 1903-1920.

Mortgage Index. Grantor/grantee, type of instrument, book and page where copy is on file, date of instrument and recording, brief legal description, alphabetical, 1903-1920.

Miscellaneous Index. Grantor/grantee, type of instrument, book and page where copy is on file, date of instrument and recording, brief legal description, alphabetical, 1903-1920.

Towns, Additions, Cemeteries. Grantor/grantee, type of instrument, legal description of property, book and page where copy is on file, chronological, 5 volumes, 1907-1920.

GRADY *COUNTIES*

Court Clerk

   Civil. Appearance docket as to any filings, number and style of case, names of attorneys, orders from the court, indexed alphabetically, volume unknown, 1907-1920.

   Criminal. Appearance docket as to any filings, number and style of case, names of attorneys, orders from the court, indexed alphabetically, volume unknown, 1907-1920.

   Marriage Records. Names and ages, indexed alphabetically, volume unknown, 1907-1920.

Election Board

   None (no records prior to 1920).

Sheriff

   None.

Superintendent of Schools

   Census Records. Name of parents, name of student, date of birth, numerically by school district, 1914-1968.

   Teachers' Contracts (incomplete). Teacher's name, hiring school, amount of pay, yearly by school district, 1914-1940s.

Treasurer

   Tax Rolls. Lists real and personal property subject to taxation, shows name and address of property owner (early years do not reflect address of property owner), description of property, school district in which located and assessment value, early years listed by township names, later years by legal description of property, personal property by school district, several hundred volumes, 1907 to date.

Grant (Medford, OK 73759)

Assessor

   Assessment Rolls. Lists of all taxable lands, city and town lots and blocks, and personal property, describes property, value per acre, total value of land,

COUNTIES *GRANT*

adjusted value, etc., alphabetical by name of property owner, 43 volumes, 1908-1920.

Board of County Commissioners

Commissioners' Proceedings. Minutes of meetings, 14 volumes, 1893 to date.

County Clerk

Commissioners' Journal. Chronological, no index, 5 volumes, 1893-1920.

Deed and Mortgage Records. Copies of actual filings, indexed by legal description, 1893-.

Numerical Index (Range Books). 1 book per township plus indexes for each city and town, chronological, 1893-1920.

Grantor and Grantee Indexes. Alphabetical index of deeds, etc., alphabetical and chronological, 1893-1920.

Court Clerk

Probate. Index, dockets and cases, chronological, alphabetical, several volumes, 1893 to present.

Civil. Index, dockets and cases, chronological, alphabetical, several volumes, 1893 to present.

Divorce. Index, dockets and cases, chronological, alphabetical, several volumes, 1893 to present.

Marriage License. Index and dockets, chronological, alphabetical, several volumes, 1893 to present.

Criminal. Index, dockets and cases, chronological, alphabetical, several volumes, 1893 to present.

Election Board

None (no records prior to 1921).

Sheriff

Jail Records. Name, charge, arrest and jail information, alphabetical, 1893 to date.

GRANT   *COUNTIES*

Superintendent of Schools

    None.

Treasurer

    Permanent Tax Rolls. Owner and legal description of the various parcels of land and lots for the entire county, amount of tax, chronological, 3-5 volumes per year, 1894 to date.

    Warrant Registers. Registration of warrants for county workers and for schools, chronological, 1900 to date.

Greer (Mangum, OK 73554)

Assessor

    Assessment Rolls. Names, personal property, real estate owned, alphabetical, 200-300 volumes, 1914 to date.

    Note: Additional records stored in Old Greer County Museum, Mangum, OK.

Board of County Commissioners

    Commissioners' Proceedings. Minutes of proceedings, includes details of matters discussed, actions taken, names of parties, and all dates, no index, volume unknown, 1886 to date.

County Clerk

    Mortgage Record. Copies of mortgages on real property, date and number of instrument, names of mortgagor and mortgagee, amount and conditions, legal description of property, date and time filed, chronological, indexed alphabetical, volume unknown, 1900 to date.

    Deed Record. Copies of deeds on real property, date and number of instrument, names of grantor, legal description of property, date and time filed, chronological, indexed alphabetical, volume unknown, 1900 to date.

    Patent Record. Names, dates and legal description of land, date and time filed, volume unknown, 1900 to date.

COUNTIES *GREER*

Court Clerk

Probate. Index, dockets and cases, chronological, 5 volumes, 1901-1921.

Civil. Index, docket and cases, chronological, 5 volumes, 1901-1921.

Misdemeanor and Felony. Index, dockets and cases, chronological, 5 volumes, 1901-1921.

Divorce. Index, docket and cases, chronological, 5 volumes, 1901-1921.

Marriage. Index, alphabetical, 5 volumes, 1901-1921.

Election Board

Voter Registration Book. Lists of voters, alphabetical, 1 ledger, 1916-.

Old Greer County Museum, Mangum, OK

Tax Roll - Greer County. Lists of taxpayers and amount paid on land and personal property, chronological, 61 volumes, 1896-1957.

Treasurers' Receipt of Warrants. Receipts for all monies paid to county employees, chronological, 1 volume, 1909-1919.

Refund Voucher Record. Itemization of vouchers written, chronological, 1 volume, 1920.

Register of Bonds. School building bonds, chronological, 4 volumes, 1915-1940.

Deeded Lands. Owner, property, date of final proof listings, chronological by township range, 1 volume, 1897-1915.

Warrant Payment Register - Greer County. Warrant, to whom issued and amount, chronological by departments, 1 volume, 1915-1918.

Sheriff

None.

Superintendent of Schools

Enumeration Records. Names, dates of birth, parents and school year, numbered by school district, volume unknown, 1912-1952.

GREER *COUNTIES*

Treasurer

Records stored in the Old Greer County Museum, Mangum, OK.

Harmon (Hollis, OK 73550)

Assessor

Records stored in the Harmon County Historical Museum, Hollis, OK.

Board of County Commissioners

Minutes (stored in the office of the County Clerk). Proceedings of meetings of county commissioners, chronological, 5 volumes, 1909-.

County Clerk

Real Estate. Grantor-grantee and legal tract indexes, chronological, 1909 to present.

Patents. Information about owner and property, chronological and legal description by township, range and section, 1909 to present.

Deeds. Information about owner and property, chronological and legal description by township, range and section, 1909 to present.

Mortgages. Information about owner and property, chronological and legal description by township, range and section, 1909 to present.

Cemetery. Names and dates, chronological and alphabetical, 1909 to present.

Court Clerk

Civil. Case number, style of case, attorneys, all pleadings, court orders and judgments, chronological, indexed alphabetical, 3 volumes, 1909-1920.

Marriage. Names, ages, dates and places of marriages, indexed alphabetical, 3 volumes, 1909-1920.

Criminal. Case number, style of case, attorneys, charge, witnesses, record of proceedings, judgment and sentence, chronological, indexed alphabetical, 1 volume, 1909-1920.

COUNTIES *HARMON*

Probate and Guardianships. Case numbers, style of case, attorneys, orders, notices, inventories, accountings and decrees, chronological, indexed alphabetical, 2 volumes, 1909-1920.

Adoption. Case number, style of case, attorneys, pleadings, notices, orders and decrees, chronological, indexed alphabetical, 2 volumes, 1909-1920.

Election Board

Precinct Registers.

Harmon County Historical Museum, Hollis, OK

Personal and Property Tax Assessments. Assessments for personal and property taxes for Harmon County, some volumes missing, by township and chronological, 88 volumes, 1909-1921.

Precinct Registration Books. 1916-1954.

Sheriff

None.

Superintendent of Schools

School Enumeration Record (Census). Name of student, date of birth, address, etc., by school district, chronological, 100s of books, 1913-1968.

School District Boundary Records. Name of school and where located, legal description, 5-10 books, 1930s-.

Teacher Employment Records. Name of teacher, schools worked, salaries, etc., 5-10 books, 1920s-.

Transcript Records. From schools that no longer exist such as Ron and Benson which were consolidated with Hollis in 1964, 1-2 books.

Treasurer

Tax Rolls. Lists of real and personal property subject to taxation, shows name and property owner, description of property, number of school district located, state equalized value, amount of tax, personal property alphabetized by names of property owner, real property by section, township and range, 236 books, 1909 to date.

HARPER

Harper (Buffalo, OK 73834)

Assessor

　　None.

Board of County Commissioners

　　Minutes (stored in the office of the County Clerk). Record of proceedings of meetings, chronological, 8 books, 1920s-.

County Clerk

　　Land Records. Transactions, patents, deeds, etc., 50 books, ca. 1900-1920.

　　Field Notes. Survey taken by county surveyors, by legal description, 1 book, no date.

Court Clerk

　　Probates. All pleadings, no exhibits, indexed alphabetically but filed numerically, 68 volumes, 1907-.

　　Civil Cases. Permanent records, typed in books up to 1977, cross-indexed but filed numerically, 74 volumes, 1907-.

　　Judgment Dockets. Listing of names, alphabetical, 4 volumes, 1907- (to when law changed to include affidavit of judgment).

　　Marriage Records. Marriage applications and licenses since statehood, cross-indexed alphabetically, 10 volumes, 1907-.

　　Divorce Records. Permanent record, divorces were filed in appearance docket book with civil cases until 1969, separate index book for divorces, alphabetical, 9 volumes, 1907-.

　　Criminal Records. Alphabetical, approximately 13 volumes, 1907- (It is unclear whether all cases were filed in County Court before part of them were transferred to District Court).

Election Board

　　None.

COUNTIES *HASKELL*

Sheriff

Sheriffs' Fee and Service Records. Docket books, alphabetical, 4 volumes, 1907-1915.

Sheriffs' Appearance. Index and dockets, alphabetical, 10 volumes, 1915 to date.

Jail Records. Docket books, chronological, 3 volumes, 1907 to date.

Superintendent of Schools

School Enumeration Record (stored in the office of the County Clerk). Name of student, date of birth, etc., by school district, chronological, 100s of books, 1912-1967.

Teacher Employment Records (stored in the office of the County Clerk). No date.

Treasurer

None.

Haskell (Stigler, OK 74462)

Assessor

None.

Board of County Commissioners

None.

County Clerk

Warranty Deeds. Index, direct and indirect, alphabetical, 2 volumes, 1905-1921.

Mortgages. Index, direct and indirect, alphabetical, 2 volumes, 1907-1921.

Miscellaneous Records. Index, direct and indirect, alphabetical, 4 volumes, 1903-1921.

Reception Records. Book, page and time, daily arrangement, 8 volumes, 1907-1921.

HASKELL COUNTIES

Court Clerk

   Civil/Divorce (filed together until 1969). Docket books and case files, index reg. and reverse, chronological and alphabetical, 1907 to present.

   Divorce. Docket books and case files, index reg. and reverse, chronological and alphabetical, 1969 to present.

   Criminal (Misdemeanor/Felony). Dockets and case files, chronological and alphabetical, 1907 to present (records for last twenty years are easy to access, prior years are difficult to access and stored in courthouse basement).

   Marriage. Marriage records arranged chronologically and alphabetically, 1907 to present (records from 1946-1954 are unavailable since this book was stolen).

   Probate. Dockets and files arranged chronologically and alphabetically, 1907 to present.

   Small Claims. Docket books and files (judgments for last five years) arranged chronologically and alphabetically, 1907 to present.

Election Board

   Election Board Meetings. Business conducted at each meeting, August 6, 1912 to May 15, 1920.

   Bond Issues and Franchises. Lists some of the companies and results of the elections, August 6, 1912 to May 15, 1920.

   Candidates for Nomination. Primary elections, candidates listed in no particular order, democratic, republican and socialist parties listed, August 6, 1912 to August 3, 1920.

   Record of Ballots Furnished. General elections, ballots issued by precinct number, election dates: November 5, 1912, November 2, 1920 and November 7, 1922.

   Abstract of Votes Cast. Primary, general and special elections, listed by precinct numbers, each office and candidate and number of votes cast for each candidate, records indicate 29 precincts, records show recount for August 6, 1912 election, August 6, 1912 to August 3, 1926.

Special Election. Election called by legislature on state questions 46, 47, 57, 58 and 60, also special election called by the Board of County Commissioners for Haskell County for the purpose of erecting a courthouse and jail, August 6, 1913.

County Register of Electors. School district numbers, date of registration, age, residence, occupation, color, politics, and registration certificate number, approximately 3,339 registered voters, May 1916.

Register of Petit Jurors. Lists jurors in no particular order, lists number of miles traveled, amount paid and the number of days of term served, May 1910-1915.

Record of Certificates of Election. Certificates issued for the general election, November 5, 1912, primary, August 6, 1917 and August 6, 1920, democratic and republican parties listed, 1912-1922.

Record of Expense of Special Election. To issue bonds to erect courthouse and jail, listed in order by precinct number, shows totals for precinct officers, printing ballots, cost of ink and pencils, and traveling expenses, salaries of election board workers, cost of election was $834.00, April 26, 1913.

Sheriff

None.

Superintendent of Schools

Teachers' Records. Names of teachers and where they taught in Haskell County's 56 dependent schools, numerically by school district, 1914-1969.

Certificate of School Enumeration. Names of parents, child, date of birth, enumerator who took census, numerically by school district, 1914-1969.

Treasurer

Tax Rolls. 1907-1921.

Hughes (Holdenville, OK 74848)

Assessor

None.

HUGHES *COUNTIES*

Board of County Commissioners

None.

County Clerk

Deeds. Hand-typed deeds from original deeds, includes name of mortgagor and mortgagee, amount, conditions, legal description of property, and date and time filed, chronological and numerical, 40 volumes, 1907-1920.

Mortgages. Hand-typed mortgages from original mortgage, includes name of grantor and grantee, amount, conditions, legal description of property, and date and time filed, chronological and numerical, 38 volumes, 1907-1920.

Miscellaneous (all instruments other than deeds and mortgages). Hand-typed instruments from original instruments, includes name of grantor and grantee, legal description, length of time if oil and gas lease, and date and time filed, chronological and numerical, 30 volumes, 1907-1920.

County Commissioners' Minute Books. Record of proceedings, amounts of warrants issued by the county, and all other business, hand-typed by office of the County Clerk, chronological, 2 volumes, 1907-1920.

Census Reports. List of people in each school district, includes name, age, birth date, handwritten by guardian, filed yearly, 1907-1920.

Court Clerk

Marriage. Index, marriage record, chronological, 8 volumes, 1907-1921.

Civil. Index, dockets and cases, chronological, 6 volumes, 1907-1921.

Probate. Index, dockets and cases, chronological, 7 volumes, 1907-1921.

Election Board

None.

Sheriff

None.

COUNTIES *JACKSON*

Superintendent of Schools

> Enumeration Records. Name of student, name of parent, date of birth, by school district and year, 1 vault, 1912-1968.

Treasurer

> Records stored in the Hughes County Historical Society, Holdenville, OK.

Jackson (Altus, OK 73521)

Assessor

> None.

Board of County Commissioners

> All permanent records stored in the office of the County Clerk.

County Clerk

> Mortgage Records. Exact copies of mortgages on real property, date of instrument, names of mortgagor and mortgagee, amount and conditions, legal description of property, and date and time filed, chronological and indexed alphabetically, 2 volumes, 1898-1920.
>
> Deed Records. Exact copies of deeds of real property, date of instrument, names of grantor and grantee, legal description of property, and date and time filed, chronological and indexed alphabetically, 5 volumes, 1888-1902.
>
> Miscellaneous Records. Type of instrument, date and time filed, exact copies of each instrument, name of grantor and grantee, legal description of property, and date of instrument, chronological and indexed alphabetically, 7 volumes, 1907-1920.
>
> Patent Records. Exact copy of patent on record, date of instrument, name of grantor and grantee, legal description of property, and date and time filed, chronological and indexed alphabetically, 5 volumes, 1903-1920.
>
> Military Discharge Records. Date and length of service, type of service, exact copy of discharge on record, and date filed, chronological and indexed alphabetically, 1 volume, 1919-1920.

JACKSON   COUNTIES

Court Clerk

    Probate. Index, dockets and cases, alphabetical, 3 volumes, 1910-1920.

    Civil. Index, dockets and cases, alphabetical, 6 volumes, 1907-1920.

    Criminal. Index, dockets and cases, alphabetical, 3 volumes, 1907-1920.

    Marriage License. Index and licenses, alphabetical, 6 volumes, 1907-1920.

Election Board

    None (no records prior to 1921).

Sheriff

    None.

Superintendent of Schools

    School Census Records. Schools attended, date of birth, name of parents, chronological, 1912-1967.

    School Board Records. Names of members, 1932 to date.

    Attendance Records.

    Note: Some maps stored in the Southern Prairie Library System, Altus, OK.

Treasurer

    None (some records could be stored in the Old Greer County Museum, Mangum, OK).

Jefferson (Waurika, OK 73573)

Assessor

    None (no records prior to 1921).

COUNTIES *JEFFERSON*

Board of County Commissioners

Commissioners' Proceedings. Minutes of proceedings, include details of matters discussed, actions taken, names of parties, and all dates, chronological, no index, 9 volumes, 1907 to date.

County Clerk

Patent and Final Receipt Records. Typed copies, date and number of instrument, names, legal description of property, date and time filed, 13 volumes, 1907-1920.

Oil and Gas Records. Typed copies of oil and gas records, date and number of instrument, names of lessors and lessees, legal description of property, date and time filed, 1907-1920.

Release Assignment on Mortgage. Typed copies of mortgages on real property, date and number of instrument, names of mortgagor and mortgagee, amount and conditions, legal description of property, date and time filed, volume number 65, 1907-1920.

Mortgage Records Federal Farm Loans. Typed copies, date and number of instrument, legal description of property, date and time filed, volume number 64, 1907-1920.

Indian Deed Records, Government Roll Indian Lands. Indian roll book with section, township and range, and the roll number of Indians in Jefferson County, volume numbers 38 and 1, 1907-1920.

Unallotted Deed Records. Volume number 32.

Miscellaneous Records. Typed copies of miscellaneous records on real property, date and number of instrument, names of grantees and grantors, legal description of property, date and time filed, volume numbers 1-17, 2, 8, 16, 22, 26, 28, 29, 39, 40, 43, 46-49, 55, 59, 61, 63 and 67, 1907-1920.

Old Deed Record. Typed copies of deed record on real property, date and number of instrument, names of grantees and grantors, legal description of property, date and time filed, volume number 18, 1907-1920.

Release of Assignment Record. Typed copies of releases of assignment on real property, date and number of instrument, names of grantees and grantors, legal description of property, date and time filed, volume numbers 1, 17, 34, 51 and 62, 1907-1920.

JEFFERSON *COUNTIES*

Release of Real Estate Mortgage. Typed copies of mortgages on real property, date and number of instrument, names of mortgagor and mortgagee, amount and conditions, legal description of property, date and time filed, 1907-1920.

Mortgage Records. Typed copies of mortgages on real property, date and number of instrument, names of mortgagor and mortgagee, amount and conditions, legal description of property, date and time filed, volume numbers 3, 4, 6, 10, 11, 15, 20, 25, 33, 36, 41, 42, 44, 53, 54, 60 and 66, 1907-1920.

Deed Records. Typed copies of deed records on real property, date and number of instrument, names of grantees and grantors, legal description of property, date and time filed, volume numbers 1, 5, 7, 9, 12, 14, 18, 19, 21, 23, 24, 27, 30, 31, 35, 37, 50, 52, 56, 57 and 58, 1907-1920.

Allotment Patent Records. Typed copies, date and number of instrument, legal description of property, date and time filed, 2 volumes, 1907-1920.

Homestead Patent Record. Typed copies, date and number of instrument, legal description of property, date and time filed, 2 volumes, 1907-1920.

Patent Records. Typed copies, date and number of instrument, legal description of property, date and time filed, 2 volumes, 1907-1920.

Court Clerk

Probate. Index, dockets and cases, chronological, 2 volumes, 1907-1920.

Civil. Index, dockets and cases, chronological, 5 volumes, 1907-1920.

Marriage License. Index and dockets, alphabetical, 4 volumes, 1907-1920.

Criminal. Index and dockets, chronological, 2 volumes, 1907-1920.

Juvenile (confidential). Index, dockets and cases, chronological, 1 volume, 1907-1920.

Election Board

None (no records prior to 1920).

Sheriff

None.

COUNTIES *JOHNSTON*

Superintendent of Schools

Scholastic Census Reports. Name and address of parent or guardian with list of school age children, date of birth, age, date census taken and the name of the census taker, booklets by school districts, 6.75 linear feet, 1915-1920.

Treasurer

None.

Johnston (Tishomingo, OK 73460)

Assessor

None.

Board of County Commissioners

Records stored in the office of the County Clerk.

County Clerk

Direct and Indirect Deed. Grantor - grantee, alphabetical, 2 volumes.

Direct and Indirect Mortgage. Grantor - grantee, alphabetical, 2 volumes.

Direct - Indirect. Grantor - grantee, alphabetical, 2 volumes.

Tract Record. Grantor - grantee, by section, township and range, 2 volumes.

Indian Roll Book. Roll number, age in 1902, blood, alphabetical and chronological, 2 volumes.

Dawes Commission Record. Allotment, section, township and range, alphabetical, 1 volume.

Court Clerk

Probate. Index, dockets and cases, chronological, 3 volumes (dockets), 1907-1920.

Civil. Index, dockets and cases, chronological, 5 volumes (dockets), 1907-1920.

Felony. Dockets and cases, chronological, 2 volumes (dockets), 1907-1920.

JOHNSTON *COUNTIES*

Election Board

None.

Sheriff

None (no records prior to 1921).

Superintendent of Schools

School Enumeration Record (Census). Name of student, date of birth, etc., by school district, chronological, hundreds of books, 1912-68.

Payroll Registers. For teachers, chronological, alphabetical, 1 book per year, 1932/33-.

Treasurer

None.

Kay (Newkirk, OK 74647)

Assessor

Assessment Rolls. Assessed value and homesteads shown on list of all personal properties and all taxable land and improvements (real estate) in all rural and city areas of Kay County, ownership carried as shown on first of year, real estate by legal description, personal property by city or township and alphabetical, microfilm, 1894-.

NOTE: The Assessment Rolls (books) are on loan to the Ponca City Library, Ponca City, OK, the Newkirk Community Historical Museum, Newkirk, OK, and the Kaw City Museum, Kaw City, OK.

Board of County Commissioners

Records stored in the office of the County Clerk.

County Clerk

Deed Record. Exact copies of deeds on real property, indexed by legal description, numerous volumes, 1893 to date.

Kaw Indian Patents. Exact copies, indexed by legal description, 1 book, 1903.

COUNTIES *KAY*

Sheriffs' Deed Record. Exact copies, indexed by legal description, 1 book, 1897.

Final Receipt Record. Exact copies, indexed by legal description, 3 books, 1895-1906.

Quit Claim Deeds. Exact copies, indexed by legal description, 2 books, 1893-1904.

Tax Deeds. Exact copies, indexed by legal description, 3 books, 1900-1909.

Cross Index Records (Deeds, Mortgages and Miscellaneous). Names, legal description, dates, book and page, alphabetical, 1893 to date.

Patents. Exact copies, indexed by legal description, 5 books, 1895.

Mortgages. Exact copies, indexed by legal description, 1895 to date.

Miscellaneous. Exact copies, indexed by legal description, numerous volumes, 1893 to date.

Reception Record. Recording information, as received, numerous volumes, 1893 to date.

Court Clerk

Marriage License Records. Names of applicants, county of residence, age of applicant at time of application, date of application, date marriage ceremony performed, names and addresses of witnesses, name of person performing ceremony, alphabetical (1 index), chronological, 13 volumes, 1893-1920.

Probate. Probate, civil and divorce records, journal entries of daily proceedings, number and style of case, names of attorneys, names of parties to lawsuit, judgments entered and orders of the court, alphabetical (1 index), chronological, 7 volumes, 1893-1920.

Criminal. Journal entries of daily proceedings, number and style of case, names of attorneys, judgments entered and orders of the court, chronological, 7 volumes, 1894-1920.

Bankruptcy Docket. Journal entries of daily proceedings, number and style of case, names of attorneys, judgments entered, orders of the court and dispositions, chronological, 1 volume, 1898-1907.

United States Criminal Appearance Docket. Journal entries of daily proceedings, number and style of case, names of attorneys, judgments entered, orders of the court, chronological, 4 volumes, 1894-1920.

Partnership Record. Style of case, names of attorneys, disposition entered, chronological, no index, 1 volume, 1894-1920.

Naturalization. Petition and records, names of applicants, orders of the court, chronological, no index, 3 volumes, 1894-1920.

Citizenship. Petition and records, declaration of intention, names of applicants, orders of the court, chronological, no index, 1 volume, 1893-1905.

Election Board

None (no records prior to 1926).

Sheriff

Jail Book (Log). Name, address, cause of commitment, date committed, who committed, etc., chronological, alphabetical, 1 book, 1898-1910.

Superintendent of Schools

Record of School District Officers, Quarterly Reports and Teachers' Examination Record Book. 1911.

Record of School District Officers, Kay County Schools. By school district number, 1909-.

Record of Teachers in Kay County Schools. 1909-1915.

Record of Exams for Common School Diploma. 1921-1945.

Record of School District Officers, Kay County Schools. Includes maps of school district boundaries and changes made, 1897.

Teachers' Record. 1897-1913.

School Enumeration Records (Census). All schools in Kay County, by school district number (1 through 106), 1897-1968.

Three Sands, Peckham and Kildare High School Transcripts. Alphabetical, ca. 1920-1939.

Teacher Retirement Records. 1940s.

Normal Institute Records. 1897-1916.

Record of Examination and Diplomas. 1916-1920.

School Funds, Valuations and County Superintendent Visits. 1897-1917.

Teachers' Registers for all Dependent Schools in County. Name of student, address, parent information and attendance reports, 1940-.

Ponca Military Transcripts. Alphabetical, 1942-1974.

Teachers' Contracts. For all teachers in dependent schools in county, alphabetical, 1920 to date.

Treasurer

Tax Rolls. List of real and personal property subject to taxation, name and address of taxpayer, account number, description of property, school district, valuation of land and improvements if taxes paid, personal taxes (alphabetical), property taxes by lot, block and addition, 345 volumes, 1894 to date.

School District Warrant Register. List to whom warrant payable, purpose, warrant number, amount of interest paid, and amount of apportionment, by date of registration, 8 volumes, 1897 to date.

Sinking Fund Investment Warrant Register. Date, to whom payable, kind of bond, amount of warrant or bond, date purchased, month when coupons payable, principal received, interest received, total amount paid and date received, by date of bonds, 4 volumes, 1818? to date.

Register of Court Warrant. Date registered, number of warrant, presented by, purpose, register number, fund issued on, amount, date paid, interest, total paid and date paid, numerical by warrant number, numerous volumes, 1895-1920.

Paving Tax and Sewer Tax. Legal description of property, amount assessed by city, if paid, amount of interest paid and date paid, listed by lot, block and addition, 8 volumes, 1928 to date.

Drainage Assessments. Assessed to land description, number of acres, assessed value, fees paid, total due and paid, date of payment, paid by whom, listed by lot, block and addition, 3 volumes, 1909-1920.

Kingfisher (Kingfisher, OK 73750)

Assessor

> Assessment Rolls. List of all taxable land, cities and towns by lot and block, rural real estate by section, township and range, personal property alphabetical by name assessed, 84 volumes, 1909-1920.

Board of County Commissioners

> Records stored in the office of the County Clerk.

County Clerk

> Deeds and Records. Indexing, payroll, Uniform Commercial Code records, tract index by legal description, 1889 to date.
>
> Land Records. Deeds, mortgages, leases and miscellaneous records, legal description, 100s of volumes, 1889 to date.
>
> Patents. Tract index, legal description, 1889 to date.
>
> Farm Census Records. Legal description by township, 9 volumes, 1900-1906.
>
> Commissioners' Journal. Minutes of meetings, includes salaries paid, 8 volumes, 1890 to date.
>
> Original United States Survey of Lands.
>
> Plat Book of Kingfisher County. Lists landowners, 1 volume, 1912.

Court Clerk

> Probate. Index, dockets and cases, chronological, indexed alphabetical, 5 volumes, 1900-1920.
>
> Civil. Index, dockets and cases, chronological, indexed alphabetical, 11 volumes, 1896-1920.
>
> Divorce. Index, dockets and cases, chronological, indexed alphabetical, 11 volumes, 1896-1920.
>
> Marriage Licenses. Index and dockets, chronological, indexed alphabetical, 6 volumes, 1900-1921.

COUNTIES *KIOWA*

Adoption. Index, dockets and cases, chronological, indexed alphabetical, 4 volumes, 1900-1920.

Criminal. Index, dockets and cases, chronological, indexed alphabetical, 3 volumes, 1896-1920.

Election Board

Records stored in the Oklahoma Museum of Election History, Oklahoma City, OK.

Sheriff

None (older records transferred to county courthouse).

Superintendent of Schools

School Enumeration Record (Census). Name of student, date of birth, etc., by school district, chronological, hundreds of books, 1900-67.

Teacher Employment Records. Certificates and exams, chronological, alphabetical, 1 book, 1909-.

School District Boundary Surveys. Maps of school districts, by legal description, 1 book, 1906-.

Annual Reports of County Superintendent. Chronological, 1 book, 1914-.

Treasurer

Tax Rolls. Legal descriptions of all land in county with assessed valuations and amount of tax, by lot and block, and section, township and range, 368 volumes, 1901 to date.

Kiowa (Hobart, OK 73651)

Assessor

None.

Board of County Commissioners

Minutes of Commissioners' Meetings. Chronological, approximately 50 books, 1901-.

KIOWA COUNTIES

Minutes of Excise Board Meetings. Chronological, approximately 10 books, 1901 to date.

County Clerk

Commissioners' Journal. Minutes of meetings, salaries paid, chronological, 1901-1920.

Land Records. Deeds, mortgages, leases, etc., 20 linear feet (books), 1901-1920.

Registration of Doctors, Dentists and Optometrists. Names, schooling and licensing, 3 books, 1901-1920.

Original United States Government Survey of Lands. 1 volume, 1874.

Plat Book of Kiowa County. Landowners, 1 book, 1913.

Court Clerk

Civil. Entries of proceedings, case numbers, style of case, names of attorneys, judgments, orders, chronological, alphabetical, 9 volumes, 1901-1920.

Probate. Entries of proceedings, case numbers, style of case, names of attorneys, orders, final accountings, chronological, alphabetical, 4 volumes, 1901-1920.

Marriage. Date, age, place, alphabetical, 7 volumes, 1901-1920.

Criminal. Entries, proceedings, case numbers, charges filed, attorneys, judgment and sentences, chronological, alphabetical, 3 volumes, 1902-1920.

Naturalization. Chronological, alphabetical, 8 volumes, 1906-1955.

Election Board

None.

Sheriff

Checkbook. For warrants issued, chronological, 1 checkbook, 1917 to date.

Note: Other records stored in courthouse basement (inaccessible).

COUNTIES *LATIMER*

Superintendent of Schools

School Enumeration Record (Census). Name of student, date of birth, etc., by school district, chronological, hundreds of books, 1913-1968.

Map. Old school districts and names, one item, no date.

Treasurer

Tax Rolls. Tax payments, legal names and addresses, by legal description and school district, numerous volumes, 1920 to date.

Latimer (Wilburton, OK 74578)

Assessor

None (no records prior to 1955).

Board of County Commissioners

Minutes of Commissioners' Meetings (stored in the office of the County Clerk). Chronological, 8 books, 1907 to date.

County Clerk

Warranty Deed. From whom, to whom and land description, chronological, 12.5 volumes, 1906-1920.

Release and Assignment. From whom, to whom and land description, chronological, 2 volumes, 1908-1920.

Tax Deeds. From county, to whom and land description, chronological, 1920 to date.

Miscellaneous. From whom, to whom and land description, if applicable, chronological, 4 volumes, 1890-1920.

Mortgages. From whom, to whom and land description, chronological, 6 volumes, 1907-1920.

Land Patents, Allotted and Homestead. From Choctaw and Chickasaw Indian Nations, to whom and land description, chronological, 3 volumes, 1906-1920. Note: Latimer County Abstract Company, Wilburton, OK has a copy of all records of the office of the County Clerk.

LATIMER *COUNTIES*

Court Clerk

Probate, Guardianship and Mental Health. Index, dockets and cases, alphabetical, 3 volumes, 1908-1920.

Civil and Divorce. Index, dockets and cases, alphabetical, 3 volumes, 1908-1920.

Criminal, Misdemeanor and Felony. Index, dockets and cases, alphabetical, 3 volumes, 1907-1920.

Marriage License. Index, dockets and cases, alphabetical, 4 volumes, 1907-1920.

Election Board

None (no records prior to 1921).

Sheriff

None.

Superintendent of Schools

School Census Records. For all schools in Latimer County, by school district and alphabetical, 1912-1968.

Treasurer

Tax Rolls. Lists of real and personal property subject to taxation, name, description of property, number of school district located, chronological and by legal description, 1907-1920.

LeFlore (Poteau, OK 74953)

Assessor

None.

Board of County Commissioners

None.

COUNTIES *LEFLORE*

County Clerk

Land Records. Deeds, mortgages, power of attorney, etc., chronological and alphabetical, approximately 100 volumes, 1907-1921.

Military Discharge. Name, age, height, complexion, military service, chronological, alphabetical, 1907-1920.

Physicians' Record. Name, license date, place, by whom, chronological, alphabetical, 1907-1920.

Reception Record. Type of instrument, grantor, grantee, fees, return address, filing date, chronological, 1907-1920.

County Commissioners' Record. All proceedings pertaining to meetings of county commissioners, chronological, 1907-1920.

Direct Name Index-Deed. Grantor, grantee, filing date, legal description, alphabetical, 1907-1920.

Direct Name Index-Miscellaneous. Date filed, grantor, grantee, legal description, alphabetical, 1907-1920.

Indirect Name Index-Deed. Grantor, grantee, filing date, legal description, alphabetical, 1907-1920.

Indirect Name Index-Miscellaneous. Grantor, grantee, date filed, legal description, alphabetical, 1907-1920.

Patent. Filing date, applicant, receiver, legal description, fee, acreage, chronological, 1907-1920.

Warranty Deed Permanent Record. Grantor, grantee, legal description, dates, chronological, 1907-1920.

Miscellaneous Permanent Record. Grantor, grantee, legal description, dates, chronological, 1907-1920.

Release Permanent Record. Grantor, grantee, legal description, dates, chronological, 1907-1920.

Quit Claim Deed Permanent Record. Grantor, grantee, legal description, date, chronological, 1907-1920.

LEFLORE *COUNTIES*

Mortgage Permanent Record. Grantor, grantee, legal description, date, chronological, 1907-1920.

Court Clerk

Probate. Index, dockets and cases, entries of daily proceedings, style of case, names of attorneys, judgments entered and orders of the court, indexed chronologically, 842 linear feet, 1897 to date.

Civil and Divorce. Daily proceedings, case number, names of attorneys, judgments entered and orders of the court, indexed chronologically, 1,280 linear feet, 1907 to date.

Note: Some records stored in the Lowry Hotel (storage building), Poteau, OK.

Election Board

None.

Sheriff

None.

Superintendent of Schools

None (no records prior to 1921).

Treasurer

Tax Rolls. Name, address, legal description, chronological, numerous books, 1907 and 1930s to date.

Lincoln (Chandler, OK 74834)

Assessor

None.

Board of County Commissioners

Records stored in the office of the County Clerk.

COUNTIES *LINCOLN*

County Clerk

Certificate of Partnership. Names of partners, partnership name and date, chronological, alphabetical, 1 volume, 1905-1920.

Military Discharge. Name, age, height, complexion, military service, chronological, alphabetical, 1 volume, 1899-1920.

Physicians' Record. Name, license date, place, by whom, chronological, alphabetical, 1 volume, 1908-1920.

County Commissioners' Record. All proceedings pertaining to meetings of county commissioners, chronological, 4 volumes, 1891-1920.

Reception Record. Type of instrument, grantor, grantee, fees, return address, filing date, chronological, 16 volumes, 1891-1920.

Direct Name Index - Deed. Grantor, grantee, filing date, legal description, alphabetical, 3 volumes, 1891-1920.

Indirect Name Index - Deed. Grantor, grantee, filing date, legal description, alphabetical, 3 volumes, 1891-1920.

Direct Name Index - Miscellaneous. Date filed, grantor, grantee, legal description, alphabetical, 3 volumes, 1891-1920.

Indirect Name Index - Miscellaneous. Grantor, grantee, date filed, legal description, alphabetical, 3 volumes, 1891-1920.

Patent. Filing date, applicant, receiver, legal description, fee, acreage, chronological, 7 volumes, 1892-1914.

Warranty Deed Permanent Record. Grantor, grantee, legal description, dates, chronological, 57 volumes, 1891-1923.

Miscellaneous Permanent Record. Grantor, grantee, legal description, dates, chronological, 62 volumes, 1891-1920.

Mortgage Permanent Record. Grantor, grantee, legal description, date, chronological, 58 volumes, 1891-1920.

Quit Claim Deed Permanent Record. Grantor, grantee, legal description, dates, chronological, 6 volumes, 1891-1920.

LINCOLN *COUNTIES*

Release Permanent Record. Grantor, grantee, legal description, dates, chronological, 14 volumes, 1891-1920.

Probate Deed. Grantor, grantee, legal description, dates, chronological, 2 volumes, 1892-1920.

Tax Deed Record. Grantor, grantee, legal description, dates, chronological, 3 volumes, 1902-1920.

Townsite Deed. Grantor, grantee, legal description, dates, chronological, 3 volumes, 1893-1903.

Railroad Right of Way. Grantor, grantee, legal description, only for Saint Louis and Oklahoma City Railroad, chronological, 1 volume, 1896-1899.

Plats, Towns and Subdivisions. Owner, surveyor, date, description, lots and blocks, chronological, alphabetical, 300+ volumes, 1891-1920.

Original Geographical Survey. All lands in Lincoln County, names of surveyors and dates, 1 volume, 1875.

Final Receipt. Applicant, receiver, legal description, acreage, fees, date filed, chronological, 2 volumes, 1892-1906.

Claim Entry. Entryman, date, legal description, acreage, chronological, 1 volume, 1893-1910.

Tract Indices. Date filed, grantor, grantee, legal description, chronological, 52 volumes, 1891-1920.

Court Clerk

Civil. Journal entries, names, names of attorneys, judges' signatures, orders of the court, court minutes, includes divorces filed before 1930, chronological, alphabetical and general index, 1891-.

Probate (Adoption, Mental Health, Incompetency and Guardianships filed with Probate Court). Instruments filed, heirs, general inventory, names of attorneys, orders of the court, court minutes, final decree, chronological, alphabetical and general index, 1893-.

Note: Approximately 5-10 probate records burned in courthouse fire in 1967.

Marriage. Licenses (some original), names, dates, ages, state of origin, one docket of Indian marriages, chronological, alphabetical, & general index, 1891-.

COUNTIES *LINCOLN*

Felony. Name, information filed, disposition, chronological, alphabetical and general index, 1892 to date.

Note: Some felony records burned in courthouse fire in 1967.

Citizenship Docket. Name, date, country of origin, alphabetical, 2 volumes, 1892 to date.

Election Board

None.

Sheriff

None.

Superintendent of Schools

School Records. Enumeration records, chronological, 1908 to date.

Treasurer

Tax Rolls. Names of owners, real estate and personal property, legal description, 204 books, 1952 to date.

Delinquent Tax Sale Book. Record of advertised delinquent taxes with description of real estate, by year, 1 book, 1957 to date.

Personal Tax Lien Docket. Record of advertised personal taxes, alphabetical by name, 1 book, 1981-1987.

Tax Receipts. Paid real estate and personal tax, names and addresses of owners, numerical, 1964 to date.

Lincoln County Teachers. Payroll records, arranged by school district and alphabetical by name, chronological, 6 boxes, 1950 to date.

Corporation Tax Rolls for Lincoln County. Billed by school districts, list of corporations in county, alphabetical, 4 books, 1956 to date.

Southwest Fire District Taxes. Taxes on real estate and personal valuation, list of property owners in Southwestern Lincoln County Fire Protection District, chronological and alphabetical, 2 books, 1987-1988.

LINCOLN *COUNTIES*

Lincoln County Income, Distribution and Financial Records. Chronological, 69 books, 1965 to date.

School District Map. Original school districts of Lincoln County, shows location of school houses, boundaries, towns and railroads, 1 map, mid-1890s.

Logan (Guthrie, OK 73044)

Assessor

None.

Board of County Commissioners

None (records stored in the office of the County Clerk).

County Clerk

Warranty Deed, Home Patents, Mortgage, Miscellaneous. Index, direct and indirect, chronological and alphabetical, 1895-.

School Records. School census showing parent or guardian name, names of children and birth dates, arranged chronologically by year and school districts, 1912-1967.

Note: Additional records stored in the Logan County Historical Society, Guthrie, OK.

Court Clerk

Civil Cases. Original instruments filed in cases, chronological and alphabetical, 162 volumes, 1907 to present.

Criminal Cases. All instruments filed and docket books, chronological and alphabetical, docket books and on microfilm, 1895 to present (also Territorial Cases dating back to September 26, 1890, and Witness Book from March 15, 1895 to February 23, 1904).

Marriage Records. Includes birth dates, addresses at time of application, etc., chronological and alphabetical, 59 volumes and 16 rolls of microfilm, December 13, 1891 to present.

Probate Records. Instruments filed in cases, chronological and alphabetical, 26 docket books and on microfilm, 1893 to present.

COUNTIES *LOGAN*

Divorce Records. 130 rolls of microfilm, June 1890 to present.

Justice of the Peace - Territory of Oklahoma Records. 1 volume, March 24, 1891-October 31, 1893.

Declaration of Intention (Citizenship). 2 volumes, June 17, 1890-April 14, 1902.

Election Board

County Commissioner Minutes (Canvass of Elections). Minutes and returns for local, county, state and national elections prior to statehood, incomplete pages, chronological, 1 volume (286 pages), 1892-1902.

County Commissioner Minutes (Canvass of Elections). Minutes and returns for local, county, state and national elections prior to statehood, incomplete pages, chronological, 1 volume (320 pages), 1904-1907.

Logan County Election Board Minutes. Minutes of meetings, incomplete pages, chronological, 1 volume (286 pages), 1908-1913.

Logan County Election Board Minutes. Minutes, record of candidates, election returns, incomplete pages, chronological, 1 volume (419 pages), 1912-1922.

County Registers of Elections. Name of registered voter, school district, date of registration, age, residence, occupation, race, color, politics, registration certificate number, incomplete pages, alphabetical by precinct, 1 volume (638 pages), 1916-1919.

Election Board Precinct Register. Register of voters for Springer Precinct, incomplete pages, alphabetical by voter, 1 volume (80 pages), 1916-1928.

Election Board Precinct Register. Register of voters for Lawrie Precinct, incomplete pages, alphabetical by voter, 1 volume (80 pages), 1916-1928.

Election Board Precinct Register. Register of voters for Guthrie Precinct 2, Ward 4, incomplete pages, alphabetical by voter, 1 volume (80 pages), 1916-1928.

Election Board Precinct Register. Register of voters for precinct 18, incomplete pages, alphabetical by voter, 1 volume (80 pages), 1916-1946.

Sheriff

Records in the office of the Court Clerk.

LOGAN *COUNTIES*

Superintendent of Schools

School Census. Name, date of birth, address, schools attended, chronological, alphabetical, 1912-1968 (new listing as School Records under County Clerk).

Teacher Register/School District Officers.

Treasurer

Tax Rolls. Lists of real and personal property, name and address of property owner, description of property, school district, value and tax amount due, personal property alphabetized, real property by legal description, approximately 80 volumes, 1892-1920.

Love (Marietta, OK 73448)

Assessor

None.

Board of County Commissioners

Records stored in the office of the County Clerk.

County Clerk

Deed Records. Land transactions, chronological, 77 books, 1903-1982.

Miscellaneous Records. All types of transactions except deed and mortgage, chronological, 403 books, 1907 to date.

Mortgage Records. Mortgage on real property, chronological, 67 books, 1907-1982.

Mineral Deeds. Land description on mineral interest, chronological, 22 books, 1935-1982.

Court Clerk

Criminal Appearance Docket. Index, docket and cases, chronological, 2 volumes, 1907-1921.

Civil Appearance Docket. Index, docket and cases, chronological, 3 volumes, 1905-1921.

COUNTIES   LOVE

Estate Fee Record (Probate). Index, docket and cases, chronological, 1 volume, 1907-1921.

Marriage Record. Index and license application, chronological, 4 volumes, 1907-1921.

Election Board

   None.

Sheriff

   None.

Superintendent of Schools

   Record of Examination of Applicants for Teachers' Certificates. Names of applicant, addresses, grades, certificate numbers, date of issuance and date of expiration, by date, 1 volume, 1910-1928.

   School District Officers. Names of school district officers, listed by district, addresses, date of election, date of expiration, numerical by school district, 1 volume, 1907-1918.

   Apportionment of School Funds. School districts, dates, school funds, county funds and federal aid, numerical by school district, 1 volume, 1908-1920.

   Record of Visits to School Districts. District number, name of teacher, and county superintendent's comments, by date, 1 volume, 1908-1919.

   Record of Assessed Valuation of School District. School district number, assessed valuation, date certified by county clerk, remarks section (levy), numerical by school district, 1 volume, 1908-1927.

   Yearbook. School census, personal property, real estate, school officers, teachers' salaries, total valuations, school district number, 8 volumes, 1919-1946.

   Descriptive Boundary of School District. Boundaries dated as early as 1907, name of district, first meeting held, name of superintendent, numerical by school district, 1 volume, 1907-1929.

   Record of Examination of Applicants for Common School Diplomas. Name of student, address, grades, name of teacher, by date, 2 volumes, 1908-1922.

Blank Certificates Used for Teacher Certificates after Completion of the Eighth Grade. Student's name, grades, issuance date, expiration date and certificate number recorded in each book, by certificate number, 3 books, 1914-1929.

Institute Record. Names of teachers, post office, school where taught in previous year, no specific order, 1 volume, 1908-1912.

Clerks' Record Book. Register of warrants and board meetings for District Number 28, by date, 2 books, 1908-1919.

Note: The office of the Superintendent of Schools has on file the original name and number of Love County Schools.

Treasurer

Tax Rolls. Lists of real and personal property subject to taxation, name of property owner, description of property, number of school district, etc., no addresses, real property (chronological), personal property (alphabetical), 1 book per year, 1908-1920.

McClain (Purcell, OK 73080)

Assessor

Records kept for 10 years.

Board of County Commissioners

Records stored in the office of the County Clerk.

County Clerk

Land Records (Real Estate and Minerals). Legal description, grantee, grantor, dates, covering patents, warranty deeds, mineral deeds, quit claim deeds, mortgages, releases of mortgages, rights of way, leases, by section, township and range, 1,259 volumes, 1891 to date.

Minutes. Proceedings of county commissioner meetings, chronological, numerous books, 1935 to date.

Court Journal, Book A, United States Court, Southern District, Purcell, Indian Territory. Miscellaneous court records, chronological, indexed, 583 pages, September 20, 1895 - January 5, 1898.

Court Journal, Book B, United States Court, Southern District, Purcell, Indian Territory. Miscellaneous court records, chronological, indexed, 537 pages, January 1898 - January 27, 1902.

Court Journal, Book C, United States Court, Southern District, Purcell, Indian Territory. Miscellaneous court records, chronological, indexed, 561 pages, March 1902 - July 1905.

Court Journal, Book D, United States Court, Southern District, Purcell, Indian Territory. Miscellaneous court records, chronological, indexed, 582 pages, November 1905 - November 1907.

Court Journal, Book E, United States Court, Southern District, Purcell, Oklahoma. Miscellaneous court records, chronological, indexed, 506 pages, November 1907 - 1909.

Probate Record, Book A, United States Court, Southern District, Purcell, Indian Territory. Probate information, chronological, indexed, 453 pages, November 1895 - September 1906.

Probate Fee, Book A, United States Court, Southern District, Purcell, Indian Territory. Chronological, 311 pages, November 1895 - October 1908.

Administrators' Book A, United States Court, Southern District, Purcell, Indian Territory. Chronological, 111 pages, September 1895 - 1907.

Inventory and Appraisements, Book A, United States Court, Purcell, Indian Territory. Inventory and appraisements, chronological, 162 pages, June 1896 - April 1905.

Execution Docket and Marshals' Returns. Executions of court orders, chronological, October 1899 - September 1926.

Judgment Docket, Civil Book A, United States Court, Southern District, Purcell, Indian Territory and Oklahoma. Alphabetical, November 1895 - 1912.

Executors' Record, Book A. Proof of will, executors' bonds and applications, chronological, 19 pages, February 1899.

Naturalization Records, Book A, United States Court, Southern District, Purcell, Indian Territory. Declaration of aliens and declaration of citizenship intent, chronological, 12 pages, 1896 - 1904.

Appearance Docket, Book A, United States Court, Southern District, Purcell, Indian Territory. Chronological, cases 1-870, June 1895 - March 1906.

MCCLAIN *COUNTIES*

Appearance Docket, Book B, United States Court, Southern District, Purcell, Indian Territory. Chronological, cases 872-1100 (84 pages), March 1906 - November 1907.

Praecipe Book A, United States Court, Southern District, Purcell, Indian Territory. List of plaintiffs and defendants, case 3s subpoenas, summons, etc., chronological, 106 pages, November 1895 - November 1907.

Guardians' Records, United States Court, Southern District, Purcell, Indian Territory. Petition for appointments of guardian, guardians' bonds, letters of guardianship and index of guardians, 125 pages, February 1898 - October 1907.

Criminal Bench Docket, Book A, United States Court, Southern District, Purcell, Indian Territory. Chronological, indexed, 209 cases (61 pages), date undetermined.

Criminal Bench Docket, Book C. Chronological, 174 pages, November 1899 - September 1908 (not inclusive).

Criminal Docket, United States Marshall, United States Court, Southern District, Purcell, Indian Territory. Lists witnesses and residence, fees, dates of warrants, etc., chronological, 293 pages, December 1894 - November 1898.

Note: These records are in the process of being approved for microfilming by the Oklahoma Historical Society, Oklahoma City, OK. Inventory of additional records had not been completed at the time of the survey.

Court Clerk

Civil. Proceedings, numerous volumes, 1906 to present.

Probate. Proceedings, numerous volumes, 1906 to present.

Divorce. Proceedings, numerous volumes, 1906 to present.

Marriage Records. Marriage licenses, 6 volumes, 1906-1920.

Note: Records such as marriage licenses before 1907 are stored in the Office of the Carter County Court Clerk, Ardmore, Oklahoma.

Election Board

None.

COUNTIES *MCCLAIN*

McClain County Museum, Purcell, OK

> County Tax Rolls. Personal property and real estate, handwritten ledgers, chronological within townships and towns, 296 books (15"x18"), 1908-1965.
>
> Blanchard Civil Records. Miscellaneous information, civil and criminal dockets, warrants, license fees, 1908-1909 marriage records, bridge blueprints, city bonds, building permits, etc., chronological, 25 books (handwritten), 1908-1981.
>
> McClain County, Oklahoma Death Records. County cemeteries, Rackley's Funeral Home records, church and family records, alphabetical within cemetery, 1 book (14,000 names), 1883-1984.
>
> McClain County Records (microfilmed in 1984 by the Church of Jesus Christ of Latter-Day Saints, Mormon Church, Salt Lake City, Utah). County marriages from 1907-1930, probate index, church and family records, funeral home records, etc., chronological and alphabetical, 6 rolls, 1880s-1984.
>
> 1878 Chickasaw Nation Annuity Rolls and 1890 Chickasaw Nation Census for Pontotoc and Pickens Counties. Lists of Chickasaw Annuity Rolls from December 1878, and 1890 (some 1889) Chickasaw Nation Census for Pontotoc and Pickens Counties, no order, pages not numbered, 1 roll.
>
> Note: Microfilm is stored in the Purcell Public Library, Purcell, OK.

Sheriff

> Sheriffs' Service. Index, service performed, by whom, amount, date, chronological, 1 volume, 1915-1927.
>
> Sheriffs' Boarding of Prisoners. Name of prisoner, when jailed, chronological, 1 volume, 1911-1930.
>
> Fees Charged and Received. Case, writ, alphabetical, 1 volume, 1907-1911.

Superintendent of Schools

> School Census (stored in the McClain County Historical Society, Purcell, OK). Name of person, school attended, date of birth, record of all dependent and independent schools existent in McClain County, chronological, 1914-.

Treasurer

> None.

McCurtain (Idabel, OK 74745)

Assessor

None (no records prior to 1920).

Board of County Commissioners

None (all records stored in the office of the County Clerk).

County Clerk

Real Estate Release and Assignment. Chronological, volumes 1-20, 1907-1920.

Miscellaneous. Chronological, volumes 1-35, 1907-1920.

Mortgage. Chronological, volumes 1-53, 1907-1920.

Patent. Chronological, volumes 1-10, 1907-1920.

Deed. Chronological, volumes 1-39, 1907-1920.

Discharge DD-214s. Chronological, volume 1, 1907-1920.

Court Clerk

Marriage. Name, age, county resident, blood test, alphabetical, 54 volumes, November 20, 1907 to date.

Divorce Docket. Name, case number, alphabetical, 9 volumes, January 1, 1947 to date.

Civil Appearance Docket. Name, case number, attorney, alphabetical, 36 volumes, November 1907 to date.

Probate. Name, case number, attorney, alphabetical, 12 volumes, March 1, 1917 to date.

Criminal Docket. Name, case number, attorney, alphabetical, 14 volumes, May 1908 to date.

Small Claims. Name, case number, attorney, alphabetical, 8 volumes, February 1969 to date.

COUNTIES *MCINTOSH*

Civil Domestic Docket. Name, case number, attorney, alphabetical, 1 volume, August 22, 1985 to date.

Traffic. Name, case number, violation, alphabetical, 30 volumes, January 1962 to date.

Election Board

None (no records prior to August 1, 1922).

Sheriff

Records stored in courthouse basement (inaccessible).

Superintendent of Schools

Enumeration Record. Name, date of birth, alphabetical, numerous volumes, 1917-1957.

School Apportionment. Apportionment of common school funds to school district, date and signed order, number of school district, amount and date filed with county treasurer, by school district, 4 volumes, 1910-1921.

Treasurer

Tax Rolls. List of real and personal property subject to taxation, description of property, number of school district located, state equalized value, chronological, 1908-1920.

McIntosh (Eufaula, OK 74432)

Assessor

None.

Board of County Commissioners

Minutes (stored in the office of the County Clerk). Proceedings of meetings of county commissioners, chronological, 1 book, 1927 to date.

County Clerk

Birth and Death Records. Chronological, alphabetical, 2 books, 1905-1920s.

MCINTOSH *COUNTIES*

Land Records. Allotment, legal description, numerous books, 1907 to date.

Court Clerk

Marriage License. Names, date of birth, alphabetical index, books, November 1907-1920.

Divorce. Daily filings, number and style of case, names of attorneys, decrees and orders of court, alphabetical index, books, November 1907-1920.

Probate. Daily filings, number and style of case, names of attorneys, decrees and orders of court, alphabetical index, books, November 1907-1920.

Misdemeanor. Daily filings, number and style of case, names of attorneys, judgment, sentences and orders of court, alphabetical index, books, November 1907-1920.

Civil. Daily filings, number and style of case, names of attorneys, journal entries and orders of court, alphabetical index, books, November 1907-1920.

Election Board

Early records stored in the Oklahoma Museum of Election History, Oklahoma City, OK.

Sheriff

None.

Superintendent of Schools

None (no records prior to 1921).

Treasurer

None.

Major (Fairview, OK 73737)

Assessor

Assessments. Assessment rolls since statehood, chronological, 1907 to date.

COUNTIES *MAJOR*

Board of County Commissioners

    Minutes (records stored in the office of the County Clerk). Proceedings of meetings of county commissioners, chronological, 2 books, 1907-1920.

County Clerk

    Land Records. County real estate by township and range, 1893 to date.

    School Census. School enumeration records, chronological, 1912-1960s.

Court Clerk

    Probate. Index, dockets and cases, chronological, 13 volumes, 1907 to date.

    District Civil. Index, dockets and cases, chronological, 21 volumes, 1907 to date.

    Criminal. Index, dockets and cases, chronological, 22 volumes, 1907 to date.

    Felony. Index, dockets and cases, chronological, 3 volumes, 1907 to date.

    Small Claims. Index, dockets and cases, chronological, 5 volumes, 1969 to date.

    Marriage. Applications and marriage record, chronological, 15 volumes, 1893 to date.

    Ministers' Credentials. Credentials enabling minister to perform marriages, chronological, 3 volumes, 1893 to date.

    Naturalization Record. Declaration of intention, chronological, 1 volume, 1908-1928.

Election Board

    None (earliest records are voter registrations from 1952. Flood destroyed earlier records).

Sheriff

    None.

MAJOR *COUNTIES*

Superintendent of Schools

Enumeration Report. Lists families, students and dates of birth, by district number, 1912-1968.

Treasurer

Tax Rolls. Real estate descriptions, landowner's name and amount of taxes paid, by legal description, 3-4 volumes per year, 1907-1920.

Tax Receipts. Landowner's name, real estate description, assessed value and amount of taxes paid, numerical order as taxes were paid, numerous books (100 receipts per book), 1907-1920.

Marshall (Madill, OK 73446)

Assessor

Assessment Rolls. Lots and blocks (towns), section - township - range (agricultural land), chronological, 1911 to date.

Board of County Commissioners

None.

County Clerk

Patent Book. Chronological, indexed alphabetical, 1903-1906.

Deed, Miscellaneous and Mortgage Books. Chronological, indexed alphabetical, 1907 to date.

Soldier's Discharge. Soldier's name, date of entry and discharge, and service rank, chronological and alphabetical, 6 volumes, 1919 to date.

Tract Index. List of all transactions pertaining to real estate, legal description by township, range, section, lot and block, chronological, 1907 to date.

Alphabetical Index. All transactions pertaining to real estate and miscellaneous, chronological and alphabetical, 1907 to date.

Physician's Register. Certificates, chronological and alphabetical, 1 volume, 1924 to date.

COUNTIES *MAYES*

Cemetery. Deeds to lots in Kingston, Oakland, and Madill Woodbury Cemeteries, chronological, 1 volume, 1918 to date.

Court Clerk

Probate. Index, dockets and cases, chronological, 1 volume, 1907-1921.

Civil. Index, dockets and cases, chronological, 4 volumes, 1907-1921.

Criminal. Index, dockets and cases, chronological, 1 volume, 1907-1921.

Election Board

Election Record Book Number 1. Ledger 6567, 1 ledger book, July 10, 1908 - November 30, 1963.

Abstract (Voting). Abstract of votes cast in Marshall County, 1 ledger book, August 6, 1912.

Sheriff

None.

Superintendent of Schools

None.

Treasurer

Tax Rolls. List of real and personal property, shows name and address of property owner, description of property and school district, chronological, by lot and block (town) and section, township and range (agricultural land), 1908 to date.

Mayes (Pryor, OK 74361)

Assessor

None (earliest records date back to 1950s).

Board of County Commissioners

Records in the office of the County Clerk.

MAYES

County Clerk

Tract Indices. All transactions pertaining to real estate, by section, township and range, 1903 to date.

Alphabetical Indices. All transactions pertaining to real estate and miscellaneous, chronological, alphabetical, 1903 to date.

Physicians' Register. Physicians' certificates, alphabetical, 1907 to date.

Soldiers' Discharge. Soldiers' discharge records, alphabetical, ca. 1919 to date.

Commissioners' Proceedings. Minutes of meetings of county commissioners, chronological, 1907 to date.

Surveyors' Records. Field notes, undetermined arrangement and dates.

Court Clerk

Civil. Index, dockets and cases, chronological, index (alphabetical), 6 volumes, 1907-1920.

County Criminal. Dockets (indexed), cases, chronological, index (alphabetical), 5 volumes, 1907-1920.

Criminal Felony. Dockets (indexed), cases, chronological, index (alphabetical), 1 volume, 1907-1920.

Marriage. Index, dockets (name, age, county of residence, application, date of marriage), chronological, index (alphabetical), 5 volumes, 1907-1920.

Minute Books. Minutes of courtroom proceedings, chronological, 3 volumes, 1907-1920.

Probate. Index, dockets and cases, chronological, index (alphabetical), 4 volumes, 1907-1920.

Election Board

None.

Sheriff

None.

COUNTIES *MURRAY*

Superintendent of Schools

Scholastic Enumeration Records. Student's name, date of birth, school district located, chronological by school district number and alphabetical for names, 1912-1968.

Mayes County Teaching Personnel. Teacher's name, where taught, years taught and salary, primarily cover dependent schools in Mayes County, chronological, 1917 to date.

Treasurer

None.

Murray (Sulphur, OK 73086)

Assessor

None.

Board of County Commissioners

Records stored in the office of the County Clerk.

County Clerk

Deed Books. 31 books, 1906 to date.

Meeting Books. Minutes of meetings of county commissioners, 18 books, 1906 to date.

Miscellaneous Books. Oil and gas leases, affidavits, releases, liens, etc., 18 books, 1906 to date.

Dawes Commission. 1 book, 1906.

Patent Records. 10 books, 1906 to date.

Court Clerk

Probate. Journal entries of daily proceedings in probate cases, number and style of case, names of attorneys, decrees (judgments) entered and orders of the court, chronological with index, appearance dockets I-IV, 1907-1929.

MURRAY   COUNTIES

Civil (Including Divorce and Adoption). Journal entries of daily proceedings, number and style of case, names of attorneys, decrees (judgments) entered and orders of the court, chronological with index, appearance dockets I-IV, 1907-1922.

Criminal. Journal entries of proceedings, number and style of case, charges, names of prosecuting and defense attorneys, orders of the court, judgments and sentences, chronological with index, criminal appearance docket, 1907-1933.

Marriage. Application for marriage license including consent where applicable, marriage license, chronological with index, volumes I and II, 1907-1933.

Election Board

None (no records prior to 1921).

Sheriff

None.

Superintendent of Schools

School District Boundary Maps. Shows school districts, chronological, 1907-1922.

Record of Examination of Applicant and Common School Diploma. Name of person, school attended, grades and year in school, chronological, 1909-1924.

Consolidation of Schools. Chronological, 1908-1932.

Quarterly reports of County Superintendent. Chronological, 1908-1913.

County Superintendents' Year Book. Names of students and schools attended, chronological, 1920-22.

Treasurer

None.

Muskogee (Muskogee, OK 74401)

Assessor

None (records kept for 15 years).

COUNTIES *MUSKOGEE*

Board of County Commissioners

    Records stored in the office of the County Clerk.

County Clerk

    Day Book (Reception Record). All instruments filed, includes deeds, mortgages, miscellaneous, etc., chronological as filed, 5 books, 1901-1907.

    Reception Books. Instruments filed, time of day, date, grantor and grantee, chronological as filed, approximately 21 volumes, 1907-1921.

    General Index - Mortgages and Liens. Alphabetical, 20 volumes, 1901-1921.

    Index - Deeds. Alphabetical, 9 volumes, 1907-1921.

    General Index - Personal Property and Deeds of Trust. Alphabetical, March - October 1901.

    Numerical Indexes - Lots and Additions. By legal description, 12 volumes, pre-1907 - 1921.

    Numerical Index - City Blocks. By legal description, 8 volumes, pre-1907 - 1921.

    Numerical Index - Outside Towns. Additions, by legal description, 6 volumes, pre-1907 - 1921.

    Rental Contracts. Mortgages, liens and miscellaneous, alphabetical, 21 volumes, 1902-1903.

    Miscellaneous. Deeds, mortgages, releases and oil and gas leases, chronological, 382 volumes, 1902-1921.

    Range Land. All conveyances on property outside of city limits, for ranges 15 through 21, by legal description, 4 volumes, prior to 1921.

    Indian Records. Cherokee and Creek allotment and homestead deeds, alphabetical, 1 index and 98 books (separate books for Cherokee records and Creek records), 1 index and 17 microfilm cartridges, ca. 1901-1912.

Court Clerk

    Civil. Civil and divorce records, chronological, 13 volumes, 1908-1921.

MUSKOGEE *COUNTIES*

Probate. Chronological, 14 volumes, 1908-1921.

Criminal. Chronological, 2 volumes, 1908-1921.

Marriage License. Chronological, 20 volumes, 1908-1921.

Election Board

All records prior to 1921 stored in the Oklahoma Museum of Election History, Oklahoma City, OK.

Sheriff

None.

Superintendent of Schools

School Census. Enumeration records, by date of birth, 1912-1921.

Treasurer

None.

Noble (Perry, OK 73077)

Assessor

Assessment rolls stored in courthouse basement (inaccessible).

Board of County Commissioners

Minutes. Proceedings of county commissioners' meetings, includes County P, chronological, 5-6 books, 1893-1920.

Road Records. Chronological and by project, 2 books, ca. 1899-1925.

Surveyors' Reports. Chronological, 2 volumes, 1899-1945.

Field Notes. Original surveys, by legal description, 1 book, 1871-1872.

Field Books. For all 21 townships, by legal description, 22 books, 1901-1982.

Plat Books. For Payne County (1907) and Noble County (1912), by legal description, 2 books, 1907 and 1912.

COUNTIES *NOBLE*

County Clerk

Patent Record Number 1. Application number for homestead and final receiver's receipt number, name of person paying filing fee, date received and legal description of homestead, mixed order (referenced by grantee index or tract record), 345 pages, 1897-1908.

Patent Record Number 2. Owner of claim, legal description and number of application and homestead certificate, mixed order (referenced by grantee index or tract record), 640 pages, May 25, 1901-1915.

Tract Record, Township 20, Range 1 West. Deeds, patents, final receipts, mortgages, leases, easements, etc., by legal description (36 sections), 1 volume, 1897-1920.

Tract Record, Township 22, Range 1 West. Deeds, patents, final receipts, mortgages, leases, easements, etc., by legal description (36 sections), 1 volume, 1897-1920.

Tract Record, Township 23, Range 1 West. Deeds, patents, final patents, final receipts, mortgages, leases, easements, etc., by legal description (36 sections), 1 volume, 1897-1920.

Tract Record, Township 24, Range 1 West. Deeds, patents, final receipts, mortgages, leases, easements, etc., by legal description (36 sections), 1 volume, 1897-1920.

Tract Record, Township 20, Range 2 West. Deeds, patents, final receipts, mortgages, leases, easements, etc., by legal description (36 sections), 1 volume, 1897-1920.

Tract Record, Township 21, Range 2 West. Deeds, patents, final receipts, mortgages, leases, easements, etc., by legal description (36 sections), 1 volume, 1897-1920.

Tract Record, Township 22, Range 2 West. Deeds, patents, final receipts, mortgages, leases, easements, etc., by legal description (36 sections), 1 volume, 1897-1920.

Tract Record, Township 23, Range 2 West. Deeds, patents, final receipts, mortgages, leases, easements, etc., by legal description (36 sections), 1 volume, 1897-1920.

Tract Record, Township 24, Range 2 West. Deeds, patents, final receipts, mortgages, leases, easements, etc., by legal description (36 sections), 1 volume, 1897-1920.

Tract Record, Townships 20 and 21, Range 1 East. Deeds, patents, final receipts, mortgages, leases, easements, etc., by legal description (36 sections), 1 volume, 1897-1920.

Tract Record, Townships 22 and 23, Range 1 East. Deeds, patents, final receipts, mortgages, leases, easements, etc., by legal description (36 sections), 1 volume, 1898-1920.

Tract Record, Township 24, Range 1 East. Deeds, patents, final receipts, mortgages, leases, easements, etc., by legal description (36 sections), 1 volume, 1897-1920.

Tract Record, Townships 21 and 22, Range 2 East. Deeds, patents, final receipts, mortgages, leases, easements, etc., by legal description (36 sections), 1 volume, 1897-1920.

Tract Record, Township 21, Range 3 East. Deeds, patents, final receipts, mortgages, leases, easements, etc., by legal description (36 sections), 1 volume, 1897 to 1920.

Tract Record, Townships 24 and 25, Range 3 East. Deeds, patents, final receipts, mortgages, leases, easements, etc., by legal description (36 sections), 1 volume, 1897-1920.

Tract Record, Township 24, Range 4 East. Deeds, patents, final receipts, mortgages, leases, easements, etc., by legal description (36 sections), 1 volume, 1897-1920.

Deed Records. Landowners of Noble County, chronological by date filed, 32 volumes, 1893-1920.

Miscellaneous Records. Powers of attorney, bills of sale, chattel mortgages, doctors' certificates from the Territorial Board of Health, leases, contracts, etc., chronological by date filed, 15 volumes, 1901-1920.

Mortgage Records 1 through 34. Property mortgaged, legal description, conditions, grantor and grantee, amount, etc., chronological by date filed, 34 volumes, November 1893-1920.

General Index of Deeds (Grantor and Grantee Cross Index for Tract Records). Grantor and grantee, date of deed and filing, book and page of deed record, and legal description, alphabetical and chronological by date filed, 2 volumes, 1893-1920.

Miscellaneous Index (Grantor and Grantee Cross Index). Grazing leases, oil and gas leases, assignments, rights of way, easements, etc., alphabetical and chronological by date filed, 2 volumes, 1893-1920.

Mortgage, Grantor and Grantee Cross Indexes. Names of grantor and grantee, date of instrument and filing, volume and page of copy of mortgage, legal description of property mortgaged, alphabetical by grantor or grantee and chronological by date filed, cross index to mortgages, volume 3, 1893-1920.

Reception Records. Instruments filed, time of day, date, grantor and grantee, chronological, 10 volumes, 1893-1920.

Court Clerk

Probate Proceedings. Journal entries of daily proceedings, number and style of case, attorney of record, wills and final decrees, chronological and alphabetical index, 17 volumes, 1896 to date.

Marriage. Names and dates of marriages taking place in Noble County, age and place of residence of applicants, alphabetical and chronological, 27 volumes, 1896 to date.

Traffic Tickets. Name, date of birth, driver's license number, alphabetical, 27 volumes, 1969 to date.

Child Support. Payments recorded for child support, amount, payer and receiver, alphabetical, 4 volumes, ?? to date.

Small Claims. Number and style of case, names of parties, judgments entered, orders of court, alphabetical, 3 volumes, 1969 to date.

Criminal Records. Number and style of case, names of defendants, daily proceedings, judgments and orders of the court, alphabetical, approximately 60 volumes, 1896 to date.

Divorce Proceedings. Number and style of case, attorneys of record, judgments and orders of the court, court proceedings, instruments filed, alphabetical and chronological, 26 volumes, 1896 to date.

Civil - Common Law. Number and style of case, attorney of record, court proceedings, instruments filed, alphabetical and chronological, 28 volumes, 1896 to date.

Adoption. Number and style of case, instruments filed, orders of the court, judgments, court proceedings, alphabetical and chronological, 24 volumes, 1907 to date.

Beer Licenses. Number, name of applicant and legal description of business, alphabetical, 4 volumes, ?? to date.

Juvenile. Number and style of case, instruments filed, court proceedings, judgments and orders of the court, alphabetical, 6 volumes, 1907 to date.

Mental Health. Number and style of case, instruments filed, court proceedings, findings of the court, alphabetical, approximately 4 volumes, 1896 to date.

Election Board

Minutes of Meetings. Chronological, 1 ledger (11 items), 1915-1929.

Notice of Change in Polling Place. 1 ledger (1 item), February 4, 1921.

Resolution of Election. 1 ledger, March 24, 1925.

Ordinance Number 13 for City of Perry. 1 ledger, March 24, 1925.

Certificates of Vote. 1 ledger.

Election Expenses Records (numerous). 1 ledger, 1915-1933.

Sheriff

Court Docket. Fines, etc., chronological, 1 book, 1933 to date.

Superintendent of Schools

School Census. Dates of birth of school age children, originally 81 school districts, approximately 81 books per year, 1912-1962.

School Registers. Grades and information on students, school districts, numerous registers, 1939-1967.

Noble County Teachers' List. Names of teachers, certificates and wages, chronological, 1 volume, 1894 to date.

Eighth Grade Examinations. Grades, school districts, 2 volumes, 1923-1956.

COUNTIES *NOWATA*

Treasurer

None (early records destroyed by leak in water main).

Nowata (Nowata, OK 74048)

Assessor

No records prior to 1951.

Board of County Commissioners

Records stored in the office of the County Clerk.

County Clerk

Deeds. Index and reception record, copies of instruments, chronological and alphabetical, book 29 to book 585, 1909-1989.

Mortgages. Index, reception record and copies of instruments, chronological and alphabetical, book 29 to book 585, 1909-1989.

Miscellaneous - Assignments and Releases of Mortgages, Etc. Index, reception record, copies of instruments, chronological and alphabetical, book 29 to book 585, 1909-1989.

Federal and State Tax Liens. Index, reception record and original instrument, chronological and alphabetical, up to book 585, ? to 1989.

Judgments. Index, reception record and copies of instruments, chronological and alphabetical, up to book 585, 1979-1989.

Liens. Index, reception record and lien file, chronological and alphabetical, 1977-1989.

Minutes. Proceedings of county commissioners' meetings, chronological, 7 volumes, 1907 to date.

Note: Records, prior to 1908, were destroyed in a fire.

Court Clerk

Marriage. Card index, dockets, alphabetical, 29 volumes, 1907 to date.

NOWATA *COUNTIES*

Probate. Index, dockets and cases, chronological and alphabetical, 13 volumes, 1907 to date.

Civil. Index, dockets and cases, indexed alphabetical and docketed chronological, 26 volumes, 1907 to date.

Criminal (Misdemeanors). Index, dockets and cases, chronological and alphabetical, 1907 to date.

Criminal (Felony). Index, dockets and cases, chronological and alphabetical, 1907 to date.

Election Board

No records prior to 1921.

Sheriff

None.

Superintendent of Schools

School Enumeration. Name of parent, name of child, date of birth, age and grade, alphabetical, 1912-1919.

Treasurer

None (no records prior to 1950).

Okfuskee (Okemah, OK 74859)

Assessor

Assessment Rolls (stored in courthouse basement). Chronological, several books, 1908-20.

Assessment Table. Used to figure assessments, one table (chart on board), no date.

Board of County Commissioners

Records stored in the office of the County Clerk.

COUNTIES *OKFUSKEE*

County Clerk

Deed Record. Exact copies of deeds on real property and minerals, date and number of instrument, names of grantor and grantee, legal description of property, and date and time filed, chronological and indexed alphabetically, 5 volumes, 1907-1920.

Mortgage Record. Exact copies of mortgages on real property, date and number of instrument, names of mortgagor and mortgagee, amount and conditions, legal description of property, and date and time filed, chronological and alphabetical, 10 volumes, 1907-1920.

Miscellaneous Record. Exact copies of miscellaneous records such as oil and gas leases, assignments, etc., date and number of instrument, names, legal description of property, and date and time filed, chronological and alphabetical, 5 volumes, 1907-1920.

Patent Records from Creek Nation. Original allotment deeds to original allottees of the Creek Nation, chronological and alphabetical, 18 volumes, 1902-1907.

Commissioners' Proceedings of Okfuskee Board of County Commissioners. Minutes of Commissioners' meetings, records of claims, and salaries of employees, chronological, 4 volumes, 1907-1920.

School Records. Full name and birthday of persons from School Census, listed under parent or guardian's name, chronological and alphabetical, 1914-1920.

Election Board

None (no records prior to 1921).

Sheriff

None.

Superintendent of Schools

School Enumeration Record (Census). Name of student, date of birth, etc., by school district, chronological, 100s of books, 1911-1968 (new listing as School Records under County Clerk).

Teachers' Employment Records. Name of teacher, school where employed, salary, etc., chronological, alphabetical, 1 volume, 1917-1939.

OKFUSKEE *COUNTIES*

Teachers' Financial Records. Salary, withholding, etc., by school district, chronological, files, 1917-68.

Treasurer

Tax Rolls. Landowner, legal description, taxes, chronological, 21 volumes, 1908-1920.

Oklahoma (Oklahoma City, OK 73102)

Assessor

None (no records prior to 1921).

Board of County Commissioners

Government Land Office Notes. United States Government Survey of Oklahoma County, chronological, 3 volumes, April 1872 - May 1873.

Road Book of Oklahoma County. Record of section line roads in Oklahoma County, chronological, 1 volume, 1891-1908.

Incorporation Papers. Incorporation papers of cities and towns in Oklahoma County, chronological, files, 1890-1920.

Surveyors' Field Books and Plans. Detailed physical descriptions of surveyed areas, chronological, numerous volumes, 1872-1920.

Easements and Deeds. Originals of documents, alphabetical and chronological, numerous filed documents, 1890-1920.

Oklahoma County Officials. List of all Oklahoma County officials since territorial days, chronological, 1889-1920.

River Survey of North Canadian. Physical description of various points along the North Canadian River, 1 volume, December 1871.

Minutes of North Canadian Drainage District Number 3. Detailed physical descriptions and solutions to drainage problems along North Canadian district number 3.

County Clerk

Deed Records. Deeds to property, chronological, 375 books, 1890-1921.

COUNTIES *OKLAHOMA*

Oil and Gas Lease Records. Oil and gas leases, chronological, 2 books, 1917-1921.

Trustees' Deed Records. Deeds, chronological, 4 books, 1891-1915.

Mortgage Records. Mortgages, chronological, approximately 180 books, 1890-1921.

Miscellaneous Records and Mineral Deed Records. Any type of instrument such as deeds, mortgages, etc., 24 books, 1890-1921.

Release Records. Release of mortgages, chronological, approximately 50 books, 1890-1921.

Court Clerk

Marriage License. Ages, dates of birth, marriage dates, early marriage records contain place of birth, chronological and indexes (semi-alphabetical), 40 volumes, 1889-1920.

Superior Court. Appearance dockets, execution dockets, civil journals and criminal journals, chronological and execution dockets (semi-alphabetical), 15 volumes, 1909-1915.

Civil. Indexes, appearance dockets, judgment dockets, execution dockets, recording journals and case files, chronological, indexes (semi-alphabetical) and case files (numerical), 193 volumes, approximately 29,932 files, 1890-1920.

Criminal. Indexes, appearance dockets, dockets, indictment records and case files, chronological, indexes (semi-alphabetical) and case files (numerical), 41 volumes, approximately 4,768 files, 1890-1920.

Probate. Appearance dockets, miscellaneous dockets, cases, recording journals, indexes, record letters and bonds, guardians' reports, appeal bond records, judgment dockets, probate journals, miscellaneous and estate bonds, record of wills, administrators' record, order appointment administrator, United States Court Journal, execution docket and court journals, chronological, indexes (semi-alphabetical) and case files (numerical), 102 volumes, approximately 7,000 files, 1890-1920.

Naturalization. Declaration of intention, petition for naturalization, first papers, second papers, chronological, 8 volumes, 1890-1920.

OKLAHOMA *COUNTIES*

Election Board

None (no records prior to 1920).

Sheriff

Criminal Arrests, Jail Detention. Lists arrests and detentions in county jail including first recorded hanging in Oklahoma County, chronological, one logbook, 1900 to date.

Superintendent of Schools

Census Records. Name of student, date of birth, date of record, names of parents and siblings, enumerator, alphabetical, chronological, 5 file cabinets (also on 42 rolls of microfilm), 1915-1962.

School District Boundaries. Books showing legal description of school district boundaries and changes, by district number, 2 books, 1900 to date.

Annexation Files. Registers all changes through annexations, by school district number, 2 file cabinets, 1900 to date.

Record of County Superintendents. List of names, years served, photographs and biographies, chronological, 17 volumes, 1890 to date.

Teachers' Registers. Books containing students' names, grades, grade attended, attendance, district number, chronological, 120 books, 1933 to date.

County Superintendents' Year Book. List of teachers and number of students in the dependent schools, alphabetical, 7 volumes, 1916-1939.

Examination Records. Eighth grade examination for common school diplomas (dependent schools), 1 volume, 1911-1917.

Annual Report and Enumeration Records. Teachers' or principals' annual report on students in the dependent schools, by district number, 21 volumes, 1891-1931.

Register of Teachers in Oklahoma County. Record of examination for teachers' certificates, alphabetical, 5 volumes, 1891-1945.

Apportionment of Funds. Apportionment of funds for dependent schools, 9 volumes, 1892-1962.

Superintendents' Annual Report. Annual report for dependent schools, 1894-1903.

COUNTIES *OKMULGEE*

County Superintendents' Year Book. Census, school officers and teachers, separate school order, 8 volumes, 1914-1939.

Certification of Teachers. Contracts and state certificates, alphabetical, 1890-.

Treasurer

Sales Worksheets. Worksheets for county sales, by account number, microfiche, 1905-1916.

November Sales. Microfiche, 1915 and 1919.

County Sales. Microfiche, 1915-1918.

Individual Sales. Microfiche, 1918, 1919 and 1920.

Oklahoma County Tax Lists (stored in the Metropolitan Library System, Oklahoma City, OK). Legal description of land, tax assessed, date of payment, name of person paying tax, chronological, 17 volumes, 1891-1899.

Railroad Tax Roll (stored in the Metropolitan Library System, Oklahoma City, OK). Tax assessments of the Southern Kansas Railway Company, Choctaw, Oklahoma and Gulf Railway, and the Pullman Palace Car Company of Oklahoma County, chronological, 3 volumes, 1891-1914.

Okmulgee (Okmulgee, OK 74447)

Assessor

None (records kept for seven years).

Board of County Commissioners

Records stored in the office of the County Clerk.

County Clerk

Land Indexes. All information indexed against land, by legal description, approximately 50 volumes, 1907 to date.

Liens. Mechanics' Liens, all judgments, Internal Revenue Service liens, Oklahoma Tax Commission judgments, alphabetical by claimant or owner, numerous volumes, ca. 1979 to date.

OKMULGEE

Reception Records. All instruments received including deeds, mortgages, miscellaneous, etc., filed as received, direct and indirect indexes, alphabetical and chronological, approximately 100 volumes, 1907 to date.

Bookkeeping, Payroll and Accounts Payable. All accounting records, payroll (confidential), chronological, 1982-1989.

Chattels. By owner, alphabetical, numerous volumes, 1979 to date.

Minutes of Boards. Commissioners' and Excise Board meetings, chronological, numerous volumes, ca. 1969 to date.

Election Board

None (no records prior to 1921).

Sheriff

None.

Superintendent of Schools

School Enumeration Record. Lists children attending school in county by family, shows age, date of birth and grade in school, chronological and alphabetical by city and rural schools, 98 books, 1914-1920.

Treasurer

None (records kept for a maximum of 16 years).

Osage (Pawhuska, OK 74056)

Assessor

Assessment Rolls. 1951 to date.

Homestead Applications. 1951 to date.

Board of County Commissioners

Records stored in the office of the County Clerk.

COUNTIES *OSAGE*

County Clerk

>Warranty Deed. Records of ownership, chronological, 31 volumes, 1906-1920.

>Quit Claim Deed. Quit claim deed records, chronological, 2 volumes, 1906-1921.

>Town Lot Record. Town lot deeds, chronological, 8 volumes, 1906-1925.

>Miscellaneous Records. All recordings other than deeds, mortgages and releases, chronological, 25 volumes, 1907-1923.

>Mortgages. Mortgages on real estate, chronological, 30 volumes, 1906-1920.

>Oil and Gas Leases. Oil and gas leases, chronological, 3 volumes, 1906-1921.

>Discharge Books. Military records, chronological, 1 volume, 1919-1920.

>Physicians' and Dentists' License Journal. Physicians' and dentists' licenses, chronological, 1 volume, 1913-1920.

>Veterinary and Osteopath Register. Register of veterinarians and osteopaths, chronological, 1 volume, 1913-1957.

>Commissioners' Journals. Commissioners' minutes, chronological, 2 volumes, 1907-1920.

Court Clerk

>Civil Cases (includes divorce cases prior to 1917). Number and style of case, names of attorneys, journal entries of daily proceedings, judgments entered and orders of the court, chronological order with indexes, 6,804 cases, 1897-1920.

>Divorce Cases. Number and style of case, names of attorneys, journal entries of daily proceedings, orders of the court and decrees, chronological order with indexes, 675 cases, 1917-1920.

>Probate Cases (includes guardianship and adoption cases prior to 1910). Style of case, name of attorney, administrator and petitioner (probate) or guardian (guardianship), recorded in paragraph form on docket pages, chronological order with indexes, 1,475 linear feet and microfilm, 1907-1920.

>Marriage Records. Names and ages of both parties, name of minister, and place of marriage, chronological order with indexes, 2,550 marriages, 1907-1920.

OSAGE *COUNTIES*

Criminal Cases. Number and style of case, name of attorney, journal entries of daily proceedings, judgements entered, and orders of the court, chronological order with indexes, 550 feet and microfilm, 1904-1920.

Mental Health and Adoption Cases (confidential). 1918-1920 (mental health), 1910-1920 (adoption).

Note: Additional records stored in the Oklahoma Department of Libraries, Oklahoma City, OK.

Election Board

None.

Sheriff

None.

Superintendent of Schools

County Superintendents' Year Book. Lists board members, teachers and their salaries, number of students transferred to district, and school budget information, by school district number, 20 volumes, 1917/18-1936/37.

Eighth Grade Graduates. Eighth grade graduates in the various county schools for a particular year, alphabetical, 5 volumes, 1908-1958.

Teacher Certificate Records. Date registered in book, teacher's name, certificate number, years in which certificate valid, type of certificate, alphabetical, 2 volumes, 1910 to date.

School District Boundary Changes. Shows changes made to original school district boundaries, by school district number, 1 volume, 1907-1922.

School District Boundaries. Shows original school district boundaries and some changes, by school district number, 1 volume, 1907 to date.

Teachers' Examinations. Lists grades of teachers in courses taken for certification, alphabetical, 1 volume, 1908-1922.

Enumeration Records. Names of parents, name of child and date of birth, signatures of parents and enumerator, and date of enumeration, no order (resident by resident), numerous volumes, 1912-1961.

COUNTIES *OTTAWA*

School District Organization/Location/Annexation. Legal description where school was located, year organized, year annexed or consolidated to another district, various names of district, by school district number, 1 pamphlet, 1907 to date.

Normal Institute Fund. Teacher's name and amount of fee paid, by school district number, 1 volume, 1908-1933.

Teachers Employed in Osage County. Shows employment information concerning teachers, chronological, 1 volume, 1909-1917.

School District Officers. Board members of county schools, by school district number, 1 volume, 1908-1920.

Treasurer

None (no records prior to 1921).

Ottawa (Miami, OK 74354)

Assessor

None.

Board of County Commissioners

Records stored in the office of the County Clerk.

County Clerk

Index File Record. List of deeds, mortgages, leases, easements, releases, assignments, etc., date filed, names of grantor/grantee, mortgagor/mortgagee, book and page where copy of instrument found, alphabetical, 4 volumes, 1896-1905.

Land Index Books. List of deeds, mortgages, leases, easements, releases, assignments, etc., date filed, names of grantor/grantee, mortgagor/mortgagee, book and page where copy of instrument found, legal description by town, subdivision or section, township and range, 15 volumes, 1895-1920.

Index to Miscellaneous Records. List of mortgages, leases, easements, assignments, etc., date of instrument, date and time filed, name of person

OTTAWA *COUNTIES*

signing instrument, and to whom signed over, book and page where copy of instrument found, legal description, chronological and alphabetical, 5 volumes, 1908-1920.

Index to Deeds. Listing of all types of deeds, date of instrument, date and time filed, grantor/grantee, book and page where instrument found, legal description, chronological and alphabetical, 7 volumes, 1895-1920.

Miscellaneous Records. Copies of instruments such as deeds, mortgages, leases, easements, releases, assignments, etc., shows book, page, date and time of recording, chronological, 119 volumes, 1895-1920.

Reception Records. Listing of deeds, mortgages, leases, easements, releases and any other instrument, name of person signing instrument, date of recording, etc., chronological, 9 volumes, 1895-1920.

Commissioners' Journal. Minutes of commissioners' meetings, chronological, 3 volumes, ca. 1920.

Minutes of Mortgages, Deeds of Trust. Date of reception, names of mortgagor/mortgagee, amount secured, when due and property mortgaged, chronological, 4 volumes, no date.

Court Clerk

Probate. Index, docket and files, alphabetical, 1907-1920.

Civil. Index, docket and files, alphabetical, 1907-1920.

Divorce. Index, docket and files, alphabetical, 1907-1920.

Marriage Records. Index and record books, alphabetical, 1907-1920.

Election Board

None (no records prior to late 1930s).

Sheriff

None.

Superintendent of Schools

School Enumeration Record (Census). Name of student, date of birth, etc., by school district, chronological, approximately 2,000 books, 1912-1968.

COUNTIES *PAWNEE*

School District Boundary Surveys (inaccessible storage). Maps.

Teachers' Employment Records (inaccessible storage).

Treasurer

None (records date back 20 years or less).

Pawnee (Pawnee, OK 74058)

Assessor

Assessment Rolls. Personal property and land, alphabetical and chronological, 350 volumes, 1912-1930.

Board of County Commissioners

Records stored in the office of the County Clerk.

County Clerk

Final Receipt. Exact copies of final receipts on real property, date and number of instrument, names, amount and conditions, legal description of property, and date and time filed, chronological and indexed alphabetically, 1 volume, 1900-1911.

Patent Records. Exact copies of patents, date and number of instrument, names of grantors and grantees, amount and conditions, legal description of property, and date and time filed, chronological and indexed alphabetically, 3 volumes, 1901-1934.

Deed Records. Exact copies of deeds on real property, date and number of instruments, names of grantors and grantees, amount and conditions, legal description of property, and date and time filed, chronological and indexed alphabetically, 80 volumes, 1894-1959.

Mortgage Records. Exact mortgage on real property, date and number of instrument, names of mortgagor and mortgagee, amount and conditions, legal description of property, and date and time filed, chronological and indexed alphabetically, 54 volumes, 1894-1984.

Oil and Gas Leases. Exact oil and gas leases on real property, date and number of instrument, names of lessors and lessees, amount and conditions, legal description of property, and date and time filed, chronological and indexed alphabetically, 32 volumes, 1913-1957.

Assignment of Oil and Gas Leases. Exact assignments of real property, date and number of instrument, names of assignors and assignees, amount and conditions, legal description of property, and date and time filed, chronological and indexed alphabetically, 19 volumes, 1917-1957.

Miscellaneous Records. Exact copies of miscellaneous records of real property, date and number of instrument, names of parties of the first part and parties of the second part, amount and conditions, legal description of property, and date and time filed, chronological and indexed alphabetically, 78 volumes, 1893-1957.

Resale Tax Deed Records. Exact copies of resale tax deed instruments, names of grantors and grantees, amount and conditions, legal description of property, and date and time filed, chronological and indexed alphabetically, 4 volumes, 1920-1956.

Cemetery Record Book. Exact copies of deeds on real property, date and number of instruments, names of grantors and grantees, amount and conditions, legal description of property, and date and time filed, chronological and indexed alphabetically, 1 volume, 1970 to present.

Record Book. Copies of all instruments filed in Office of Real Property, date and number of instruments, names of grantors and grantees, amount and conditions, legal description of property, and date and time filed, chronological and indexed alphabetically, 487 volumes, 1957 to present.

Federal Tax Lien Records. Exact copies of federal tax liens filed, date and number of instruments, names of parties involved, amount and conditions, and date and time filed, chronological and indexed alphabetically, 3 volumes, 1925 to present.

Judgment Records. Exact copies of judgments filed, date and number of instruments, names of parties involved, amount and conditions, and date and time filed, chronological and indexed alphabetically, 3 volumes, 1979 to present.

Court Clerk

Probate. Index, dockets and cases, alphabetical, 3 volumes, 1897 to date.

Marriage. Index and dockets, alphabetical, 3 volumes (index), 1897 to date.

COUNTIES *PAYNE*

Civil and Divorce. Index and cases, alphabetical, 6 volumes (index), 1897 to date.

Election Board

None.

Sheriff

None.

Superintendent of Schools

School Census Records. Name, sex, age, date of birth, parent or guardian of students for ages 6 through 20, by school district, numerous books, 1912-1968.

Teachers' Register. Shows teachers employed in the schools of Pawnee County, type of certificate held, salary, school taught and number of months in school term, chronological, 22 volumes, 1917-1968.

Eighth Grade Examination Records. Names, dates and grades of those who took the eighth grade examination, primarily chronological, 3 volumes, 1915-1968.

Permanent Grade Records. Permanent grades of Quay, Maramec, Blackburn, and Jennings High School students, chronological, numerous books and file cards, 1920-1968.

County Superintendents of Pawnee County. List of all county superintendents and dates served, chronological, 1 book, 1893 to date.

Annexation and Consolidation Records. Various records of annexations and consolidations of Pawnee County schools, primarily chronological, 1 filing cabinet drawer, 1912-1988.

Treasurer

Tax Rolls. 4 volumes, 1906 to date.

Payne (Stillwater, OK 74074)

Assessor

None.

PAYNE *COUNTIES*

Board of County Commissioners

Minutes (stored in the office of the County Clerk). Proceedings of county commissioners' meetings, chronological, 2-3 books, 1895-1920.

County Clerk

Patent. Original title of property, grantors/grantees, legal description, date and time filed, chronological, indexed alphabetical, 6 volumes, 1895-1907.

Deed Records. Transfers of title to real property, grantors/grantees, date documentary stamps, legal description, date and time filed, chronological, indexed alphabetical, 57 volumes, 1895-1920.

Mortgages. Mortgages on real property, date and number, grantors/grantees, amount, conditions, legal description, date and time filed, chronological, indexed alphabetical, 57 volumes, 1894-1920.

Miscellaneous Records. All instruments not falling within the above mentioned, decrees, court orders, rights of way, grantor/grantee, legal description, date and time filed, chronological, indexed alphabetical, 19 volumes, 1895-1920.

Release Records. Instruments releasing mortgages, liens, leases, etc., grantors/grantees, legal description, date and time filed, chronological, indexed alphabetical, 24 volumes, 1901-1920.

Assignments Records. Assignment of rights or any interest in property, a majority of the records concern the assignment of mineral interests and leases, grantors/grantees, legal description, date and time filed, chronological, indexed alphabetical, 11 volumes, 1905-1920.

Lease Records. Leasing of mineral interest, grantors/grantees, terms and conditions, legal description, date and time filed, chronological, indexed alphabetical, 13 volumes, 1912-1920.

Court Clerk

Civil/Probate/Divorce/Felony/Misdemeanor/Small Claims/Traffic. All court cases filed relating to the various types of proceedings, chronological and alphabetical, 750 volumes, 1900-1994.

Civil/Probate/Divorce/Felony/Misdemeanor/Small Claims/Traffic. All court cases filed relating to the various types of proceedings, computer docketed, 1994 to present.

COUNTIES *PITTSBURG*

Note: Additional records are stored at the Community Center.

Election Board

Registered Voters and Election Results. By townships, 12 books, 1902-1965.

Sheriff

None.

Superintendent of Schools

School Enumeration Record (Census). Name of student, date of birth, etc., by school district, chronological, 100s of books, 1911-1968.

Treasurer

Tax rolls (stored in the Sherrar Museum, Stillwater, OK).

Bank Books. 1890s-1920.

Warrants. 1900 to date.

Maps. 1930s.

Pittsburg (McAlester, OK 74501)

Assessor

None (records kept for 10 years).

Board of County Commissioners

None.

County Clerk

Deeds. Transfer of property, chronological, 87 volumes, 1907-1921.

Mortgage. Lien on property, chronological, volume number 40, 1907-1921.

Assignment and Release. Release of mortgage, assignment and transfer, chronological, volume number 19, 1907-1921.

Miscellaneous. Oil and gas leases, mortgages and assignments, instruments other than deeds, chronological, volume number 15, 1907-1921.

Numerical Index. Indian land allotted before statehood, volume number 4, 1902-1907.

Patent, Miscellaneous and Deed. Alphabetical, volumes A - Z, 1907-1921.

Court Clerk

Marriage License. Application, blood test, copy of license in book, marriage license recorded, chronological, indexed alphabetical, 14 volumes, 1907-1920.

Probate, County Court. Journal entries, daily posting, number and style of case, names of attorneys, judgments entered and orders of court, chronological, indexed alphabetical, 5 volumes, 1907-1920.

Naturalization Records. Petition (name, country left, port entered and ship), affidavit (name, trade, oath of allegiance, order of court, admitting petitioner, and certificate of naturalization number), declaration of intention (personal identification such as name, age, etc., country left, when left and ship), alphabetical in chronological order (no index to some of the older dockets), 15 volumes, 1916-1924.

Ministers' Credentials. Name, church in which ordained, members of ordination board, revocation, chronological, 4 volumes, 1890-1920.

Criminal. Number and style of case, names of attorneys, charges, daily posting of judgments, entered court orders, posting of cost, chronological, indexed by defendant's name, 2 volumes, 1909-1920.

Superior Court. Entered court order and judgment, style of case and number, names of attorneys, clerk fees, journal entries, daily proceedings, chronological and cross index, 2 volumes, 1910-1914.

Civil. Entered court order and judgment, style of case and number, names of attorneys, clerk fees, journal entries, daily proceedings, chronological and cross index, 2 volumes, 1909-1920.

Bench Dockets. All court orders set out by judge, gives style and information about case, no index, 8 volumes, 1907-1920.

Mental Health. Original documents, dockets include number and style of case, all daily entries including judgments, alphabetical in chronological order, 5 drawers, 1908-1921.

COUNTIES *PITTSBURG*

Juvenile. Style, case number, entries on docket such as daily posting of pleadings, judgments and orders, alphabetical in chronological order, 5 drawers (2 dockets), 1910-1920.

Adoption. Number, style, entries of judgment and pleadings, alphabetical (under child's original name) in chronological order, 2 volumes, 1908-1920.

Note: All records prior to 1907 are stored in the Oklahoma Historical Society, Oklahoma City, OK. The Oklahoma Historical Society is scheduled to prepare microfilm of the records so that user copy microfilm is available at the office of the Court Clerk.

Election Board

None (no records prior to 1958).

Pittsburg County Genealogical and Historical Society, McAlester, OK

Note: The following records are available on microfilm.

United States District Court, Second Division, South McAlester, Indian Territory.

Tribal Citizenship and Probate Records.

Records. June 1890 - June 1892, and September 1890 - September 1891.

Common Record. Book 3, January 29, 1892 - January 27, 1893; book 4 January 27, 1893 - October 13, 1893; and books 5 through 12.

Probate Records. Guardians' Record A and B, and Administrators' Record A.

United States District Court, Central Division, South McAlester, Indian Territory.

Marriage Records. Volumes 7 through 13.

Naturalization Records.

Census Records, etc.

1896 Census of Choctaw Nation.

1893 Chickasaw Payment Roll.

PITTSBURG *COUNTIES*

1896 and 1897 Chickasaw Census.

1878 and 1890 Census of the Chickasaw Nation, Indian Territory.

1902 Record of Choctaws.

1855 Census of Choctaws in Indian Territory.

1902 Index of Rejected Applicants, Indian Rolls.

1885 Moshlatubbe District Census, Choctaw Nation.

1910 Census of Choctaw Nation, Creek Nation, and Chickasaw Nation, Indian Territory.

1885 Index of Indian Territory Census.

1910 Census for Pittsburg County, Bryan County, Beckham County, Blaine County, and Payne County.

Tobucksy, Towson and Wade Court Records, 1876-1904.

Note: The following records are available in hard copy.

Pittsburg County Cemeteries List.

Chaney Funeral Home Records from 1905.

1920 Pittsburg County School Records.

Pittsburg County Land Plats.

Church Register, First Presbyterian Church, Hartshorne, OK.

Sheriff

Prisoner Books. Description of prisoners, chronological, 2 books, 1911-20.

Superintendent of Schools

Scholastic Enumerations. Name of child, and parent or guardian, date of birth and age at time of enumeration, signature of parent or guardian, chronological and by school district, 1920- (records prior to 1920 were destroyed in a courthouse fire).

COUNTIES *PONTOTOC*

Treasurer

None.

Pontotoc (Ada, OK 74820)

Assessor

None (no records prior to 1920).

Board of County Commissioners

Minutes (stored in the office of the County Clerk). Proceedings of county commissioners' meetings, chronological, books, 1939 to date.

County Clerk

Patents (Homestead, Freedman, Allotment and Townsite). Patent-original deeds given to the Choctaw and Chickasaw Nations, by date of recording, numerous books, pre-1907 to date.

Deeds, Mortgages and Miscellaneous Recordings. Land records from pre-statehood through present, by date of recording, pre-1907 to date.

Court Clerk

County Misdemeanor and Traffic. Charges, pleadings, court minutes, judgment and sentences, district attorney, defense attorney and presiding judge, indexed alphabetically, chronological order by case number as filed, dockets 1 through 3, 1907-1920.

County Criminal. Charges, pleadings, court minutes, judgment and sentences, district attorney, defense attorney and presiding judge, indexed alphabetically, chronological order by case number as filed, dockets 1 thru 4 (records on microfilm), 1907-1920.

County Civil. Petition, all pleadings and journal entry of judgment if entered, attorneys involved and presiding judges, judgment dockets reflecting all judgments entered, filed chronologically, indexed and cross-indexed, dockets 1 thru 9 (records on microfilm), 1907-1920.

County Probate, Judicial Determination and Conservatorship. Petition, all pleadings and journal entries, attorneys involved and presiding judges, filed chronologically, indexed and cross-indexed, dockets 1 thru 12 (records on microfilm), 1907-1920.

Marriage License. Marriage licenses contain date of birth and/or age of applicants, witnesses to the marriage, minister or justice of the peace officiating, and date married, issued and recorded, filed chronologically, indexed and cross-indexed, dockets 1 thru 7 (also on microfilm), 1907- 1920.

Adoption Records (confidential). All records pertinent to an adoption, require order from judge to open to inspection, indexed alphabetically, 1 volume, 1907-1920.

Juvenile Records (confidential). Require judge's order to open to inspection, indexed alphabetically, 1 volume, 1907-1920.

Mental Health (confidential). All information regarding persons with mental problems, indexed alphabetically, volumes 1 thru 3, 1907-1920.

Election Board

None.

Sheriff

No records dating back to 1920.

Superintendent of Schools

School Census Records. Shows name of student, date of birth, color, sex, name of parent and enumerator, chronological and by school district number, numerous books, 1912-1968.

Treasurer

None.

Pottawatomie (Shawnee, OK 74801)

Assessor

None (records stored in the office of the County Clerk).

COUNTIES *POTTAWATOMIE*

Board of County Commissioners

None.

County Clerk

Mortgage. Grantor, grantee, land description, date of sale, purchase, etc., chronological, 146 books, February 27, 1892 - January 9, 1953.

Oil and Gas Lease. Grantor, grantee, land description, dates, chronological, 16 books, August 12, 1904 - October 31, 1929.

Miscellaneous. Include various instruments, grantor, grantee, land description, dates, chronological, 353 books, February 13, 1892 - March 24, 1959.

Warranty Deed. Grantor, grantee, land description, dates, chronological, 194 books, August 2, 1895 - January 12, 1953.

Tax Deed. Grantor, grantee, land description, dates, chronological, 2 books, November 25, 1895 - November 29, 1907.

Trustees' Deed. Grantor, grantee, land description, dates, chronological, 2 books, January 20, 1892 - March 9, 1892.

Note: Duplicate copies of some of the records of the office of the County Clerk are available at the Pottawatomie County Historical Society, Shawnee, OK.

Court Clerk

Probate. Wills and heirs, chronological and indexed alphabetically, 4 volumes (indexes), 1892 to present.

Criminal-Felony/Misdemeanor. Offenses, judgment and sentence, chronological and indexed alphabetically, 2 volumes (indexes), 1892 to present.

Civil and Small Claims. Law suits, amounts and judgments, chronological and indexed alphabetically, 1892 to present.

Divorce. Decrees, information on child support and settlement, chronological and indexed alphabetically, 1892 to present.

Election Board

None (consult the Oklahoma Museum of Election History, Oklahoma City, OK).

POTTAWATOMIE *COUNTIES*

Superintendent of Schools

Teacher Examinations. Scores of teacher applicants, chronological, one volume, 1891 to date.

Original School Board Members. District numbers and office holders, chronological, 1 volume, 1891.

Original Plat Book of School Districts. Legal descriptions of original districts, chronological, 2 volumes, 1891.

School Apportionment and School Warrant Registers. Financial records, chronological, several volumes, various dates to 1891.

Treasurer

Tax Rolls. 159 volumes, ca. 1896-1920.

Pushmataha (Antlers, OK 74523)

Assessor

None.

Board of County Commissioners

Minutes (stored in the office of the County Clerk). Proceedings of meetings of county commissioners, chronological, 2 books, 1907-1920.

County Clerk

Index. Deeds, mortgages, miscellaneous, alphabetical, 1907 to date.

Tract. Land descriptions, by section, township and range, 1907 to date.

Court Clerk

Civil and Divorce. Index, dockets and cases, chronological, 2 volumes, 1907-1921.

Probate. Index, dockets and cases, chronological, 2 volumes, 1907-1921.

Felony and Misdemeanor. Index, dockets and cases, chronological, 1 volume, 1907-1921.

COUNTIES *ROGER MILLS*

Marriage. Chronological and alphabetical, 4 volumes, 1907-1921.

Election Board

None.

Sheriff

None.

Superintendent of Schools

School Enumeration Record (Census). Name of student, date of birth, etc., by school district, chronological, numerous books, 1934-1968.

Note: No records prior to 1934 due to courthouse fire.

Treasurer

None.

Roger Mills (Cheyenne, OK 73628)

Assessor

None (all records prior to 1921 destroyed).

Board of County Commissioners

Commissioners' Proceedings. Minutes of proceedings, includes details of matters discussed, actions taken, names of parties and all dates, chronological, no index, 4 volumes, 1892-1920.

County Clerk

Patents. Filed information, copies and or printed forms of instrument, lessor/lessee, description of land, chronological, indexed alphabetically, 9 volumes, 1884-1920.

Quit Claim Deeds. Copies of deeds of lessor/lessee, description of land, filing information, chronological, indexed alphabetically, 2 volumes, 1895-1920.

ROGER MILLS COUNTIES

Warranty Deeds. Deeds of lessor/lessee, description of land or property, filing information, dates, etc., chronological, indexed alphabetically, 30 volumes, 1892-1920.

Leases/Oil and Gas Leases. Lessor/lessee, copies of property, terms of lease, legal description, dates of instrument and filings, chronological and alphabetical, 3 volumes, 1897-1920.

Mortgages. Lessor/lessee, legal description, terms of mortgage, filing dates, date of instrument, chronological, alphabetical, volume 11 and 30, 1892-1920.

Court Clerk

Civil. Civil number, type of case, attorney names, petition, entry of appearance, orders, notices, summons, journal entry and judgments, index and cross-index, 6 volumes, 1894-1920.

Probate. Deceased person's name, decree of settlement, names of attorneys, all documents filed in the case, index, 2 volumes, 1907-1920.

Felony. Person's name, charge, judgment and sentence, attorney's name, index, 3 volumes, 1892-1920.

Misdemeanor. Person's name, charge, judgment and sentence, attorney's name, index, 2 volumes, 1909-1920.

Marriage. Names of persons, ages, residences, witnesses and who officiated, index, 5 volumes, 1893-1920.

Election Board

Precinct Register. Registration of voters, alphabetical and chronological, 3 volumes, 1916-1950.

Election Board Meetings and Precinct Records. Chronological, 1 volume, 1916-1949.

Abstract of Election Returns. Chronological, 1 volume, 1910-1928.

Election Returns. Chronological, 1 volume, 1892-1924.

Sheriff

Jail Register. For County F, Oklahoma Territory, and Roger Mills County, alphabetical, 1 volume, 1893-1953.

COUNTIES *ROGERS*

Superintendent of Schools

School Enumeration Record (Census). Name of student, date of birth, etc., by school district, chronological, 100s of books, 1918-1968.

Treasurer

None.

Rogers (Claremore, OK 74017)

Assessor

None.

Board of County Commissioners

Minutes (stored in the office of the County Clerk). Proceedings of county commissioners' meetings, chronological, numerous books, 1907-1920.

County Clerk

Deed Record. Exact copies of deeds on real property, date and number of instrument, names of grantor and grantee, legal description of property, date and time filed, chronological and alphabetical, 1907 to date.

Mortgage Record. Exact copies of mortgages on real property, date and number of instrument, legal description, amounts, date and time filed, chronological and alphabetical, 1907 to date.

Miscellaneous Records. Exact copies of instruments, names of grantor and grantee, legal description, date and time filed, chronological and alphabetical, 1907 to date.

Federal Tax Liens. Exact copies of instruments, name of debtor, amounts and type of tax, date and time filed, chronological and alphabetical, 1907 to date.

Tax Warrants. Exact copies of instruments, name of debtor, amounts and type of tax, date and time filed, chronological and alphabetical, 1907 to date.

Judgments. Exact copies of instruments, name of debtor and creditor, case number, chronological and alphabetical, 1907 to date.

ROGERS *COUNTIES*

Servicemen Discharges. Exact copies of instruments, names of servicemen, alphabetical, March 18, 1919 to date.

Court Clerk

Probate. General index to records of probate cases and civil cases, index number 1, 1907-1926.

Civil. Index number 1, 1907-1926.

Marriage. Marriage licenses, dockets, alphabetical (both names), 49 dockets, 1907 to date.

Election Board

Election Record. Handwritten names, occupations, addresses, ages, voter registration, by precinct location, 4 ledger books, 1914-1956.

Election Record. Record of minutes of election board, chronological, 1 ledger book, 1914.

Sheriff

None.

Superintendent of Schools

School Census Records. Names of parents or guardians, school district, name of child, date of birth, age, chronological and by school district number, approximately 3,575 volumes, 1911-1967.

School Districts. Legal descriptions, chronological and by school district number, 1 volume, 1907.

Teacher Testing. For Craig, Nowata, and Rogers Counties, date tested, money received from institute fund, chronological, 1 volume, 1909-1913.

Public School Funds Apportionment. Chronological and by district number, 1 volume, 1919-1920.

Note: Some records stored in the Rogers County Historical Society, Claremore, OK.

COUNTIES *SEMINOLE*

Treasurer

None.

Seminole (Wewoka, OK 74884)

Assessor

None.

Board of County Commissioners

Records stored in the office of the County Clerk.

County Clerk

> Patents and Territorial Deeds. Exact copies of deeds of real estate, date and number of instrument, grantor and grantee, legal description, date and time filed, chronological and alphabetical, books 1 through 6, pre-1907.
>
> Deeds. Same as above, direct and indirect indexes by last name, alphabetical and numerical, books 1 through 1621, 1907 to date.
>
> Mortgages. Same as above, direct and indirect indexes by last name, alphabetical and numerical, books 1 through 1621, 1907 to date.
>
> Miscellaneous. Same as above, also includes mineral related instruments, oil and gas leases, and final decrees, judgments or other filings relating to real estate, direct and indirect indexes by last name, alphabetical and numerical, books 1 through 1621, 1907 to date.
>
> Mechanics' and Materialmens' Liens. Exact copies of liens, date and number of lien, legal description, date and time of filing, lien claimant and to whom filed against, numerical and alphabetical, books 1 through 25, 1978 to date.
>
> Money Judgments and Oklahoma Tax Warrants. Exact copies, amount of judgment, date and time filed, judgment debtor and judgment creditor, numerical and alphabetical, books 1 through 6, 1978 to date.
>
> Military Discharge Records. Exact copies, name of service person, date of filing, alphabetical, books 1 through 20, ca. 1919 to date.
>
> Uniform Commercial Code Filings. Mortgages of personal items, household goods, boats, cattle, etc., other than real estate, alphabetical, several file

SEMINOLE   *COUNTIES*

cabinets, records kept 10 years (some filings continued under new number and date).

Proceedings of County Commissioners, Excise and Equalization Boards. Description of county business transacted while in session, chronological (date of meeting), numerous books, 1907 to date.

Court Clerk

Marriage Records. Applications and verifications of marriages, alphabetical, November 1907 to date.

Civil. Index, docket and cases, alphabetical, 1915 to date.

Probate. Index, docket and cases, alphabetical, 1909 to date.

Guardians' Record. Index and docket, alphabetical, November 1907 - February 1923.

Criminal. Index, docket and cases, alphabetical, 1907 to date.

Election Board

None.

Sheriff

None (no records prior to 1978).

Superintendent of Schools

Census. Date of birth, names of parents, where born, school district attended, for students aged 6 through 18 years old, chronological and by school district, 2,040 books, 1910-1950.

School Records. Record of all students in school, grades, parents, dates, chronological, 6,000 names, 1910-1950.

Teachers' Contracts. Records of all teachers in various school districts, chronological, 800 items, 1910-1945.

Maps. All school districts, chronological, 200 items, 1910 to date.

Annexations. Additions to school districts, chronological, 300 items, 1910 to date.

COUNTIES *SEQUOYAH*

Treasurer

None (no records prior to 1921).

Sequoyah (Sallisaw, OK 74955)

Assessor

None.

Board of County Commissioners

None.

County Clerk

Land Records. Deeds and mortgages, chronological and by section, township and range, 60 volumes, 1907-1920.

Birth Records. Birth information as filed by doctor or midwife, chronological and alphabetical, 5 volumes, 1907-1917.

Death Records. Death information as filed by doctor, chronological and alphabetical, 5 volumes, 1907-1917.

Official Bond Records. Person bonded and amount of bond, chronological, 2 volumes, 1907-1919.

Military Discharge Records. By date of filing, 1 volume, 1918-1919.

Court Clerk

Civil. Dockets, indexes, cases and journals, chronological, 5 dockets, 5 journals and approximately 10 associate dockets, December 2, 1907 - December 1921.

Probate. Dockets, indexes, cases and journals, chronological, 4 dockets, 4 journals, and approximately 45 associate dockets, November 1907 - December 1921.

Criminal. Dockets, indexes, cases and journals, chronological, 3 dockets and approximately 15 associate dockets, November 1907 - December 1921.

Full Blood Records. Docket, index and cases, chronological, 1 docket, no date.

SEQUOYAH *COUNTIES*

Election Board

None.

Sheriff

None.

Superintendent of Schools

None (no records prior to 1925).

Treasurer

None (records kept for 10 years).

Stephens (Duncan, OK 73533)

Assessor

None.

Board of County Commissioners

None (records stored in the office of the County Clerk).

County Clerk

Deed Records. Grantor-Grantee, legal description, filing data, handwritten and typed copies, dates of instruments, chronological, 31 volumes, 1907-1920.

Allotment, Town and Homestead Patent Records. Indian roll numbers, to whom conveyed, filing data, handwritten copies, dates of instruments, legal description, chronological, 7 volumes, 1906-1909.

Miscellaneous Land Records. Releases of mortgages, oil and gas leases, various instruments other than deeds and mortgages, grantee-grantor, filing data, handwritten and typed copies, legal description, dates of instruments, chronological, 50 volumes, 1906-1920.

Mortgage Records. Mortgagee-Mortgagor, amounts, conditions, legal description, filing data, dates of mortgages, handwritten and typed, chronological, 23 volumes, 1907-1920.

COUNTIES *STEPHENS*

Soldier Discharge Records. Service records, dates of service, date of discharge, filing data, typed copies, alphabetical, 1 volume, 1919-1920.

Commissioners' Records. Minutes of the Stephens County Commissioners' meetings, handwritten and typed, dates of meetings, business transacted for the county, claims paid, chronological, 2 volumes, 1907-1920.

Court Clerk

Divorce. Case number, style of case, nature of action, names of attorneys, orders of court, chronological, 6 volumes, 1907-1920.

Civil. Case number, style of case, nature of action, names of attorneys, orders of court, chronological, 6 volumes, 1907-1920.

Felony. Case number, style of case, nature of action, names of attorneys, orders of court, names of bondsmen, chronological, 2 volumes, 1907-1920.

Probate. Case number, style of case, nature of action, names of attorneys, orders of court, chronological, 2 volumes, 1907-1920.

Misdemeanor and Traffic. Case number, style of case, nature of action, names of attorneys, orders of court, names of bondsmen, chronological, 4 volumes, 1907-1920.

Marriage. Name of parties, ages, residences, chronological, 6 volumes, 1907-1920.

Election Board

None (no records prior to 1920).

Sheriff

Arrest Records. Arrest records in file jackets, alphabetical, 12 file cabinets, 1968 to date.

Superintendent of Schools

School Enumeration. Date census was taken, school district number, parent or guardian, name of student, date of birth, age, name of enumerator, chronological and by school district number, alphabetical by student's last name, 6 file cabinets (3" x 5" cards), 1912-1968.

STEPHENS *COUNTIES*

Listing of Teachers for Stephens County Schools. Name of teacher, certification number, salary, degree, chronological, 1 volume, 1912-1913 and 1920 to date.

Note: The original school enumeration books are stored in the Genealogical Library, Duncan, OK.

Treasurer

None (no records prior to 1964).

Texas (Guymon, OK 73942)

Assessor

None (Texas County Courthouse burned around 1926).

Board of County Commissioners

Records stored in the office of the County Clerk.

County Clerk

Land Records. Include reprinted copies of documents, indexes, reception records, etc., with the exception of certain burned records, legal description and alphabetical by grantor and grantee, 1889 to date.

Commissioners' Minutes. Proceedings, chronological, 12 volumes, 1907 to date.

Court Clerk

Felony Criminal Appearance Docket Number 1. Numerical case listing, defendant, charges, attorneys, list of instruments filed, alphabetical index and numerical by case number, case numbers 1 to 521, November 22, 1907 - October 3, 1931.

Information Record Number 1 (Felony). Numerical case listing, felony information, alphabetical index and numerical by case number, July 27, 1908 - November 1, 1920.

Information Record Number 2 (Felony). Numerical case listing, felony information, alphabetical index and numerical by case number, December 2, 1917 - February 6, 1950.

Appearance Docket Number 1 (Civil and Criminal - Hooker Division). Civil cases - numerical listings, criminal (misdemeanor) cases - numerical listings, alphabetical index and numerical by case number, case numbers 1 to 220, July 19, 1909 - June 8, 1965.

Trial Docket Criminal Number 1. Civil, trial, date docket listing case, style of case, hearing date, alphabetical index, case numbers 1 to 898, 1907-1930.

Indictment Record Number 1. Non-numerical listing of indictments, cases and information, alphabetical index, March 25, 1908 - December 15, 1910.

Civil and Criminal Docket. 1/2 civil and 1/2 criminal, journal entries and fee schedule, alphabetical index, case numbers 90 to 289, April 1, 1909 - August 11, 1911.

Trial Docket Criminal Number 1. Numerical civil case listing with judges' orders, style of case, and listing of attorneys, alphabetical index and numerical by case number, case numbers 1 to 789, 1908-1913.

Criminal Journal Number 1 (Court Minutes). Listed by month, day and year, daily written court minutes, style of case, civil and criminal, written instruments such as journal entries, judgments and sentences, orders confirming, etc., no index, March 16, 1908 - August 12, 1914.

Criminal Journal Number 1 (Probate Minutes, Civil and Criminal). Written jury term docket by month and year of term, listing of jurors and precincts, jury verdicts and case disposition, no index, December 4, 1907 - July 11, 1915.

Civil and Criminal Journal Number 1. Written jury term docket by month and year of term, listing of jurors and precincts, jury verdicts and case disposition, no index, June 25, 1909 - March 22, 1944.

Civil and Criminal Trial Docket Number 1 (Hooker Division). Title, attorneys, case status, and judges' orders, non-consecutive numerical listings, alphabetical index, 1910-1914.

Misdemeanor Criminal Appearance Docket Number 1. Defendant, charge, attorneys, listing of instruments filed, alphabetical index, case numbers 1 to 584, November 29, 1907 - January 17, 1921.

Information Record Number 1 (Misdemeanor). Misdemeanor information, complaints and indictments, alphabetical index, case numbers 11 to 515, February 4, 1908 - March 26, 1921.

Information Record Number 2 (Misdemeanor). Information, no index, case numbers 11 to 593, February 4, 1908 - March 26, 1921.

Bond Record Number 1, Administrator's Bond. Executors', administrators' and guardians' bonds, no index, July 1, 1915 - December 10, 1954.

Miscellaneous Bond Record Number 1 (Hooker). Miscellaneous bond information, alphabetical index, June 8, 1908 - February 6, 1922.

Miscellaneous Bond Record Number 1 (District Court). Miscellaneous bond information, alphabetical index, June 20, 1908 - April 5, 1912.

Miscellaneous Bond Record Number 1. Miscellaneous bond information, no index, March 9, 1908 - February 13, 1935.

Miscellaneous Bond Record Number 2. Non-numerical bond information, no index, May 5, 1912 - September 19, 1918.

Miscellaneous Bond Record Number 3. Non-numerical bond information, no index, October 12, 1918 - May 13, 1925.

Appearance Bond Record Number 1. Non-numerical listing of criminal bonds' information, alphabetical index, March 7, 1908 - March 24, 1931.

Appearance Bond Record Number 1. Non-numerical listing of criminal bonds' information, alphabetical index, March 11, 1908 - December 24, 1930.

Deputy Clerks' Record of Fees Earned and Collected Number 1. Monthly record of fees collected with listing of case style and number, 1909- 1915.

Court Journal Number 1. Miscellaneous typed information, December 18, 1916 - September 13, 1918.

Jurors' Record Number 1. Jury term listing of jurors' names, addresses, dates appearing for service, dates of filing receipts and dates of attendance, November 19, 1915 - May 19, 1933.

Fee Record Number 1. Listing style of case and fee charged, monthly report of fees collected and fees earned but not collected, no alphabetical index, 1907-1911.

Fee Record Number 1. Monthly listing of date, kind of case, case number, amount charged and amount collected, 1911-1915.

Register of Claims Number 1. Listing of creditors in individual estates with amounts allowed by administrator and amounts allowed by court, alphabetical index, January 16, 1908 - February 2, 1953.

Co-Partnership Register. Alphabetical listing of names of companies with listing of names of partners and where recorded, alphabetical, June 30, 1909 - May 7, 1965.

Mechanics' Lien Record Number 1. Alphabetical listing by name of owner, with name of claimant, date filed, description of property and amount claimed, remarks, alphabetical, January 7, 1908 - May 13, 1950.

Widows' Pension Record Number 1. Numerical case numbers, names of petitioners with petition, order, journal entry and notice with proof of publication, alphabetical index and numerical by case number, case numbers 1 to 98, June 6, 1917 - January 31 1950.

Execution Docket Number 1. Alphabetical listing of judgment debtors, with judgment creditor, date of judgment, case number, amount of judgment, costs, date of execution, county issued to, sheriff's return, alphabetical, March 27, 1907 - May 6, 1933.

School Supplies Record Number 1. Alphabetical listing, when filed, names of co-partnership or corporation, principal officer, post office, nature and character of firm or corporation, remarks, alphabetical, 1908-1933.

Insanity Record Number 1. Numerical listing of case numbers of sanity records, alphabetical index and numerical by case number, case numbers 1 to 46, April 2, 1908 - February 28, 1923.

Lunacy Record Number 1. Numerical listing of case numbers of sanity records, alphabetical index and numerical by case number, case numbers 1 to 159, August 9, 1917 - May 27, 1947.

Notarial Commission and Book Record Number 1. Individual notary information per page, alphabetical index, November 27, 1907 - February 21, 1929.

Juvenile Record Number 1. Numerical case numbers, juvenile case information, alphabetical index, case numbers 1 to 97, June 15, 1909 - March 16, 1935.

Marriage Record (Hooker Division) Number 2. Marriage application, license and certificate, alphabetical index, August 14, 1909 - June 30, 1945.

Marriage Record Number 1. Marriage application, license and certificate, alphabetical index, November 24, 1907 - April 3, 1914.

Marriage Record Number 2. Marriage application, license and certificate, alphabetical index, April 15, 1914 - January 19, 1921.

Judgment Docket Number 1 (Hooker Division). Alphabetical listing by judgment debtor with date of judgment, creditor, amount of judgment, remarks, when satisfied, alphabetical, 1908-1952.

Judgment Docket Number 1. Alphabetical listings by judgment debtor, with date of judgment, creditor, amount of judgment, remarks, and when satisfied, alphabetical, 1908-1916.

Judgment Docket Number 2. Alphabetical listing by judgment debtor, with date of judgment, creditor, amount of judgment, remarks and when satisfied, alphabetical, 1916-1926.

Judgment and Execution Docket Number 1. 1/2 judgment docket, 1/2 execution docket, alphabetical listing by judgment debtor, with date of judgment, creditor, amount of judgment, remarks and when satisfied, alphabetical, July 27, 1910 - April 24, 1945.

Ministers' Credentials Record Number 1. Ministers' credential information, alphabetical index, chronological filing, January 5, 1910 - September 5, 1956.

Foreign Process Book Number 1. Numerical listing of date received, county received from, type of process, case number, style of case, date delivered to and returned from sheriff, date returned to county, fee information, alphabetical index, March 12, 1919 - March 18, 1976.

Civil Appearance Docket Numbers 1, 2, 3 and 4. Numerical case numbers, style of case, action, attorneys, list of instruments filed, case numbers 1 to 2,447, alphabetical index, 4 volumes, November 22, 1907 - February 7, 1921.

Civil General Indexes. Plaintiff and defendant, alphabetical listing of parties and case number, alphabetical, 1 volume (plaintiff) and 1 volume (defendant), 1907-1938.

Civil Appearance Docket Number 4. Style of case, course of action, listing of instruments filed in case, and fees, alphabetical index, May 19, 1907 - December 20, 1910.

Journal Civil Number 1 (Minutes, County Court). Judges' minutes and yearly jury term information, list of jurors, attorneys, etc., no index, November 21, 1907 - June 6, 1947.

COUNTIES *TEXAS*

Civil Appearance Docket Number 2. Style of case, cause of action, attorneys, listing of instruments filed and fees, alphabetical index, case numbers 148 to 1064, January 5, 1911 - July 31, 1944.

District Civil Journal Numbers 2, 3 and 4. Typed civil information, no index, daily filings, 4 volumes, July 10, 1909 - May 19, 1922.

Trial Docket Civil Number 1. Trial docket status, case numbers, title, attorneys, status of case or previous orders, judges' orders, case numbers 1 to 870, 1908-1929.

Civil Trial Docket Number 3. Trial docket status, case numbers, title, attorneys, status of case or previous orders, judges' orders, 1917-1919.

Probate Appearance Docket Numbers 1 and 2. Style of case, attorneys, listing of instruments filed, case numbers 1 to 1181, alphabetical index, 2 volumes, November 20, 1907 - December 31, 1931.

Probate Journal Numbers 1 and 2. Typed probate instruments, by filing date, 2 volumes, July 6, 1915 - June 7, 1923.

Probate Record Number 1 (Hooker Division). Typed probate instruments, by filing date, May 28, 1915 - March 29, 1937.

Probate Minutes Numbers 3 and 4. Handwritten probate instruments, February 15, 1912 - October 6, 1913.

Probate Trial Docket (Transfer). Numerical case numbers, style of case, attorneys, daily listing of instruments filed in case, alphabetical index and numerical by case number, case numbers 33 to 665, September 10, 1908 - August 9, 1921.

Administrators' Record Number 1. Order for hearing, petition for letters of administration, order appointing administrator, letters of administration, alphabetical index, February 12, 1908 - March 24, 1915.

Administrators' and Executors' Record Number 1. Record of executors and administrators with will annexed, order for hearing petition for probate of will, deposition of subscribing witness, record of will, administrators' and executors' bonds, alphabetical index, December 14, 1907 - May 1, 1915.

Guardians' Record Number 1. Guardians' records, order for hearing petition for appointment of guardian, order appointing guardian, letters of guardianship, guardians' bonds, alphabetical index, case numbers 6 to 218, January 7, 1908 - June 4, 1914.

TEXAS *COUNTIES*

Election Board

None (no records prior to 1921).

Sheriff

None.

Superintendent of Schools

Scholastic Census Records. Name of student, date of birth, name of school, name of father, and date of enumeration, numerical by school district number, 53 drawers, 1915-1968.

History of Early Schools. Map of district, names of board of education members, names of teachers, teachers' salaries, number of students and reports of superintendents' visits, for 20 of 143 schools, numerical by school district, 1 volume, 1908 to date.

Treasurer

Ad Valorem Taxes for Texas County. Includes owners' names, legal description and taxes paid, by school district, 6 volumes, 1907-1920.

Ad Valorem Taxes for Texas County. Tax roll of public service corporations, includes legal description and taxes paid, by school district, 1 volume, 1907-1920.

Tillman (Frederick, OK 73542)

Assessor

Assessment Rolls. List of taxable land and town lots and blocks, assessed value of land and improvements, legal description, 25 volumes, partial listing prior to 1921.

Board of County Commissioners

Records stored in the office of the County Clerk.

County Clerk

Miscellaneous Record. All recordation regarding land tracts, includes deeds, mortgages, assignments, leases, oil records, etc., photocopies (black with white

COUNTIES *TILLMAN*

lettering, very dim and brittle), difficult to copy, chronological, book 69 to book 124, 1917-1921.

Miscellaneous Record. All recordation regarding land tracts, deeds, mortgages, assignments, leases, oil records, etc., transcriptions made before photocopying available, chronological, approximately 68 volumes, 1907-1917.

Minutes. Proceedings of meetings of county commissioners, chronological, files, 1952-.

Court Clerk

Civil Cases. Petitions, journal entries, names of attorneys, daily entries of proceedings, case numbers, orders of the court, indexed in each book, master index, alphabetical, 5 volumes, November 1907-1920.

Probate Cases. Final decrees, listing of heirs, date of death, orders of the court, chronological order of filing, alphabetical index in each book and master index, 1 volume, 1907-1920.

Criminal, Felony and Misdemeanor. Information, charges, court orders, journal entries, alphabetical index in each book and master index, 4 volumes, 1907-1920.

Divorce. Names, court orders, decrees and family members, chronological order of filing, alphabetical index in each book and master index, 5 volumes, 1907-1920.

Marriage Records. Applications and marriage licenses, alphabetical index in each book and master index, 6 volumes, 1907-1920.

Immigration and Citizenship. Names, mode of transportation, and country of origin, chronological, 1 volume, 1907-1920.

Election Board

Proceedings of the Tillman County Election Board. Names of candidates for the board, length of terms, votes cast, condition of roads, length of time before election boxes returned, etc., chronological, 1 volume, 1910-1962.

Sheriff

None (no records prior to 1960).

TILLMAN *COUNTIES*

Superintendent of Schools

>School Census. School district number, names of parents, names of children, ages, alphabetical, 100 volumes, 1912-1969.

Treasurer

>Tax Rolls. Alphabetical and legal description, 4 volumes, 1907 to date.

Tulsa (Tulsa, OK 74100)

Assessor

>Assessment Rolls. Real estate in Tulsa County, alphabetical, 1 volume, 1908.

>Assessment Rolls. Indian allotment sections, Tulsa County, alphabetical, 1 volume, August 2, 1908 - January 1, 1909.

>Assessment Rolls. Fry Township, Tulsa County, alphabetical, 1 volume, 1910.

>Assessment Rolls. Lynn Lane number 1, alphabetical, 1 volume, 1910.

>Township, Range and Section Book. Pertaining to Indian land, alphabetical, 1 volume, 1899.

Board of County Commissioners

Records stored in the office of the County Clerk.

County Clerk

>Tract Index. Grantor/grantee, dates, book and page, and legal description of all real estate records on property listed (first filed), alphabetical, 1 book, 1907 to date.

>Grantor/Grantee Index. Buyer/seller, date of document, date filed, book and page, 1907 to date.

>Allotment Deed. From Creek Nation or Cherokee Nation to individuals, alphabetical, book and page, 1903-1907.

>Miscellaneous Index. Items before county commissioners, alphabetical and chronological, 27 books (large), 1907 to date.

COUNTIES *TULSA*

Journals. Minutes of county commissioners' meetings, chronological, 51 books (large), 1907 to date.

Court Clerk

Criminal. Felony/misdemeanor cases, chronological, 9 microfilm cartridges, 1911-1921.

Probate, Wills and Guardianships. All original documents in estate proceedings and guardianships, chronological, 1906-1920.

District Court. All original documents in civil, divorce and name change proceedings, chronological, 1906-1920.

Criminal. Appearance docket sheets, dates and minutes of proceedings, chronological, 1906-1920.

Election Board

None (no records prior to 1930s).

Note: Some early voter registration records stored in the Tulsa Genealogical Society, Tulsa, OK.

Sheriff

None (no records prior to July, 1926).

Superintendent of Schools

State Certificate Register. Listing of teachers, kind of teaching certificate and date issued, chronological, 1 volume, 1925-1930 (includes some issue dates prior to 1921).

School District Officers. Name and date elected, board position, district, chronological, 1 volume, 1908-1940.

Examination for Teacher Certificate. Name, age, city, number of weeks of attendance at school, experience as teacher, present standing in each area, certificate number, grade of certificate, date of issue and expiration, chronological, 1 volume, 1908-1928.

Record of Examination of Applicants for Common School Diplomas. Name, address, date of examination, age, district number, years of work completed, grade in each subject, and name of teacher, chronological, 1 volume, 1908-1920.

Register of Teachers Employed. Name of teacher, post office address, grade of certificate, district number, salary, and opening and closing dates of school on some records, chronological, 1 volume, 1909-1928.

Record of Teachers' Certificates Issued. Name, number, date of issue, date of expiration, and grade of certificate, chronological, 1 volume, 1908-1928.

School District Boundaries. Date laid out and organized, legal description, and date first meeting held, chronological, 1 volume, 1907-1933.

Treasurer

None.

Wagoner (Wagoner, OK 74467)

Assessor

None (no records prior to 1921).

Board of County Commissioners

Records stored in the office of the County Clerk.

County Clerk

Deeds. Land records (transfer property), alphabetical, 150 books, 1906-1920.

Mortgages. Mortgages, alphabetical, 150 books, 1906-1920.

Transcripts. Deeds of trust, rental contracts, warranty deeds, mortgages, miscellaneous filings, etc., typewritten, chronological, 5 books, 1905-1921.

Commissioners' Records. Proceedings of county commissioners' meetings, chronological, 4 books, 1907-1921.

Land Indexes. Land descriptions, buyers, sellers, mortgages, leases, etc., chronological, 20 books, 1906-.

COUNTIES *WASHINGTON*

Court Clerk

Probate. Index, dockets and cases, chronological, 1 volume, 1907-1920.

Civil. Index, dockets and cases, chronological, 3 volumes, 1907-1920.

Election Board

None (no records prior to 1921).

Sheriff

None.

Superintendent of Schools

School Enumeration Record (Census). Name of student, date of birth, etc., by school district, chronological, 100s of books, 1917-1968.

Treasurer

None.

Note: Some records stored in the Carnegie Library, Wagoner, OK.

Washington (Bartlesville, OK 74003)

Assessor

Assessment Rolls. Real estate, by legal description, chronological, 4 volumes per year, ca. 1912-1920.

Board of County Commissioners

Minutes (stored in the office of the County Clerk). Proceedings of county commissioners' meetings, chronological, microfiche, 1907 to date.

County Clerk

Real Estate Records. Index, grantor-grantee, 100s of books (also on microfiche, and January 1995 to present are computerized), ca. 1903 to date.

WASHINGTON *COUNTIES*

Key to Enrollment of Citizens of Cherokee Nation. Allotments of land, arranged by legal description (township, range and section), 7 volumes, August 1, 1908-December 31, 1908.

Election Board

None.

Sheriff

None.

Superintendent of Schools

School Enumeration Record (Census). Name of student, date of birth, etc., by school district, chronological, 100s of books, 1922-1968.

Treasurer

Records stored in courthouse attic (inaccessible).

Washita (Cordell, OK 73632)

Assessor

Washita County Tax Assessment Roll. Assessment (cities), New Cordell, Dill City, Bessie, Sentinel, Foss and Rocky, chronological, 6 volumes (1 volume per city), 1920.

Washita County Tax Assessment Roll. Assessment (townships), Cordell, Bessie, Rainey, Texas, Union, Seger, Oak Dale, Turkey Creek and Elk, chronological, 9 volumes (1 volume per township), 1920.

Washita County Tax Assessment Roll. Assessment (cities), Sentinel, New Cordell, Bessie, Dill City, Rocky and Foss, chronological, 6 volumes (1 volume per city), 1919.

Washita County Tax Assessment Roll. Assessment (townships), Oak Dale, Bessie, Texas, Seger, Rainey, Elk, Cordell, Union and Turkey Creek, chronological, 9 volumes (1 volume per township), 1918.

Washita County Tax Assessment Roll. Assessment (cities), New Cordell, Bessie, Sentinel, Rocky, Dill City and Ross, chronological, 6 volumes (1 volume per city), 1917.

COUNTIES *WASHITA*

Washita County Tax Assessment Roll. Assessment (townships), Bessie, Texas, Seger, Union, Cordell, Elk, Turkey Creek, Rainey and Oak Dale, chronological, 9 volumes (1 volume per township), 1917.

Washita County Tax Assessment Roll. Assessment (cities), Bessie, New Cordell, Rocky, Foss, Dill City and Sentinel, chronological, 6 volumes (1 volume per city), 1916.

Washita County Tax Assessment Roll. Assessment (townships), Bessie, Seger, Elk, Turkey Creek, Rainey, Union, Texas, Cordell and Oak Dale, chronological, 9 volumes (1 volume per township), 1916.

Washita County Tax Assessment Roll. Assessment (cities), Dill City, Bessie, New Cordell, Sentinel, Foss and Rocky, chronological, 6 volumes (1 volume per city), 1915.

Washita County Tax Assessment Roll. Assessment (townships), Cordell, Texas, Bessie, Oak Dale, Seger, Turkey Creek, Elk, Rainey and Union, chronological, 9 volumes (1 volume per township), 1915.

Washita County Tax Assessment Roll. Assessment (cities), Sentinel, Dill City, Bessie, Rocky, New Cordell and Foss, chronological, 6 volumes (1 volume per city), 1914.

Washita County Tax Assessment Roll. Assessment (townships), Oak Dale, Union, Bessie, Turkey Creek, Elk, Rainey, Seger, Texas and Cordell, chronological, 9 volumes (1 volume per township), 1914.

Washita County Tax Assessment Roll. Assessment (cities), Dill City, Bessie, Sentinel, Oak Dale, Foss, and Cordell, chronological, 6 volumes (1 volume per city), 1913.

Washita County Tax Assessment Roll. Assessment (townships), Elk, Turkey Creek, Bessie, Rainey and Seger, chronological, 6 volumes (1 volume per township), 1913.

Washita County Tax Assessment Roll. Assessment (cities), Cordell, Sentinel, Rocky and Bessie, chronological, 4 volumes (1 volume per city), 1912.

Washita County Tax Assessment Roll. Assessment (townships), Turkey Creek, Texas, Oak Dale, Elk and Rainey, chronological, 5 volumes (1 volume per township), 1912.

Washita County Tax Assessment Roll. Assessment (townships), Seger and Elk, chronological, 2 volumes (1 volume per township), 1911.

WASHITA

Washita County Tax Assessment Roll. Assessment, Sentinel (city), Seger (township) and Elk (township), chronological, 3 volumes (1 volume per city/township), 1910.

Washita County Assessment Roll. Assessment (township), Rainey, chronological, 1 volume, 1907.

Washita County Tax Assessment Roll. Assessment (townships), New Cordell and Rainey, chronological, 2 volumes (1 volume per township), 1906.

Washita County Tax Assessment Roll. Assessment (city), Cordell, chronological, 1 volume, 1905.

Washita County Tax Assessment Roll. Assessment (townships), Elk, Bessie and Turkey Creek, chronological, 3 volumes (1 volume per township), 1904.

Washita County Tax Assessment Roll. Assessment (township), Cordell, chronological, 1 volume, 1902.

Washita County Tax Assessment Roll. Assessment (township), Union, chronological, 1 volume, 1901.

Washita County Tax Assessment Roll. Assessment (townships), Union, Cloud Chief and Elk, chronological, 3 volumes (1 volume per township), 1900.

Washita County Tax Assessment Roll. Assessment (township), Cloud Chief, chronological, 1 volume, 1898.

Washita County Tax Assessment Roll. Assessment (townships), Union, Cloud Chief and Elk, chronological, 3 volumes (1 volume per township), 1897.

Washita County Tax Assessment Roll. Assessment (townships), Korn Valley, Oak Dale and Cloud Chief, chronological, 3 volumes (1 volume per township), 1896.

Record of School District Officers. Names of officers in school district, chronological by district, 1 volume, 1893-1903.

Board of County Commissioners

Minutes (stored in the office of the County Clerk). Proceedings of county commissioners' meetings, chronological, 2 books, 1892-1920.

COUNTIES *WASHITA*

County Clerk

> Land Records. Legal description, 1907 to date.
>
> School Enumeration. Name of student and school, 1914-1968.
>
> School Teachers' Records. Name of teacher and school where taught, 1915-1957.

Court Clerk

> Probate. Entries of daily proceedings, number and style of cases, names of attorneys, judgments and orders entered, chronological, alphabetical index, 4 docket books, 1903-1920.
>
> Marriage. Names of applicants, ages, places of residence, races, names of parents, date of marriage, places of birth, chronological, alphabetical index (some cross-indexed), 10 docket books, 1892-1920.
>
> Civil/Early Divorce (Combined). Entries of daily proceedings, number and style of cases, names of attorneys, judgments and orders entered, chronological, alphabetical index, 7 docket books, 1892-1920.
>
> Immigration/Naturalization. Declarations of intention include name of applicant, city and county of origin and/or place of birth (occupation, physical description, place of residence, name of port/station, name of sailing ship/railroad line and date of arrival in the United States in some volumes), chronological (some alphabetically indexed), volume undetermined, ca. 1893-1920.
>
> Immigration/Naturalization. Certificates of naturalization include name, age, name of court, county and state which issued declaration, and names, ages and place of residence of wife and children, date of order, chronological, volume undetermined, ca. 1911-1920.

Election Board

> Precinct Record Index. Alphabetical, 16 volumes, 1921 and prior years.

Sheriff

> None.

Superintendent of Schools

> Records kept in the office of the County Clerk.

WASHITA *COUNTIES*

Treasurer

None.

Woods (Alva, OK 73717)

Assessor

None.

Board of County Commissioners

School Census and Records. Names of teachers, students, parents and officers, issuance of teacher certificates, and plats of school boundaries, chronological, 1894-1920.

County M Surveyor Records. Original surveyor notes and cornerstone locations, chronological, 5 volumes, 1872-1921.

County M School Superintendent Notes. Brief descriptions of visits to rural schools, chronological, 1 volume, 1897-1921.

Note: Additional records stored in the Cherokee Strip Museum, Alva, OK.

County Clerk

Final Receipts. Name of grantee and land description, chronological, 8 volumes, 1903-1927.

Patent Records. Name of grantee and land description, issued by United State Government, chronological, 12 volumes, 1908-1920.

Mortgage Records and Indexes. Names of mortgagor and mortgagee, land description, date and time of filing, chronological and alphabetical, approximately 65 volumes, 1894-1920.

Reception Records. Date and time of filing, type of instrument, names of grantor and grantee, chronological, 15 volumes, 1895-1920.

Grantor/Grantee Indexes (Direct and Indirect). Names of grantor and grantee on deeds, alphabetical, 14 volumes, 1894-1920.

Deed Records. Names of grantor and grantee, description of property, date and time of filing, chronological, approximately 73 volumes, 1894-1920.

Commissioners' Proceedings. Minutes of meetings include claims and warrants approved, etc., chronological, 3 volumes, 1893-1920.

Delinquent Tax Sales. List of property for delinquent taxes, taxpayer's name and description of property, chronological, 5 volumes, 1908-1920.

Miscellaneous Records. Tax deed record (1 volume), tax deed of land bid (1 volume), trustee's deed (2 volumes), resale tax deed (1 volume), sheriff's deed (1 volume) and quit claim deed (1 volume), chronological, 7 volumes, 1894-1920.

Note: The following listings are of County M records.

Patent Records. Name of grantee and land description, issued by United States Government, chronological, 2 volumes, 1902-1908.

Deed Records. Names of grantee and grantor, description of property, reception date and time, chronological, 4 volumes, 1899-1908.

Numerical Land Indexes. For Woodward County now Woods County, and Woods County now Alfalfa County and Major County, chronological, volume undetermined, 1894-1908.

Miscellaneous. Powers of attorney, appointments, judgments, bills of sale, physicians' certificates, etc., chronological, 1 volume, 1894-1908.

Court Clerk

Marriage. Marriage licenses, names, dates, places of residence, chronological, 2 volumes, 1890 to date.

Probate. Probate cases, chronological, 1890 to date.

Misdemeanor. Cases, names, dates of offenses, chronological, 1890 to date.

Felony. Names, dates of offenses, chronological, 1890 to date.

Civil. Names, dates and kinds of cases, chronological, 1890 to date.

Note: Additional marriage license records stored in the Alva Public Library, Alva, OK.

Election Board

None.

Sheriff

Photographs. Sheriffs and deputies, 2 prints, 1902 and 1926.

List of Sheriffs. Names of sheriffs of Woods County and M County, alphabetical, 1 item, 1893 to date.

Notice to Taxpayers. Includes names of tax collectors, 1 item, 1901.

Letterheads from Sheriffs. 1894 and 1900 to date.

Jail Book. 1 book, 1894-1917.

Court Records (stored in basement). Names, court dates, etc., volume and dates undetermined.

Superintendent of Schools

Records stored in the office of the Board of County Commissioners.

Treasurer

Tax Rolls. Chronological, about 80 books, ca. 1899-1920.

Woodward (Woodward, OK 73801)

Assessor

None (no records prior to 1921).

Board of County Commissioners

Minutes (stored in the office of the County Clerk). Proceedings of county commissioners' meetings, chronological, 4 books, 1893-1920.

County Clerk

Grantor/Grantee Deed Books. List of instruments, date of filing, date of instrument, type of instrument, and book and page where recorded, alphabetical, volume 1 through 25, 1894 to date.

Grantor/Grantee Mortgage Books. List of instruments, date of filing, date of instrument, type of instrument, and book and page where recorded, alphabetical, volume 1 through 12, 1894 to date.

Grantor/Grantee Miscellaneous Book. List of instruments, date of filing, date of instrument, type of instrument, and book and page where recorded, alphabetical, volume 1 through 25, 1894 to date.

Deed Records. Copies of deeds recorded in Woodward County, name of grantor/grantee, date recorded, legal description of property being sold and/or transferred, numerical arrangement, volume 1 through 98, 1894-1951.

Mortgage Record and Miscellaneous Record. Mortgage record books cover all mortgages recorded through 1951, grantor/grantee, date recorded and legal description of property being sold and/or transferred, miscellaneous record books contain mortgages and other instruments dated 1951 to date, numerical arrangement, volume 1 through 84 (mortgage record books), and volume 1 through 1,140 (miscellaneous record books), 1894 to date.

Tract Index Books. Legal description (section, township and range), Woodward County ranges 17 through 22, chronological, prior to 1907-1989.

Court Clerk

Marriage License. Chronological, 4,522 cases (12 drawers), 1897-1920.

Criminal. Misdemeanor and felony, chronological, 813 cases (15.5 drawers), 1895-1920.

Probate. Guardianship, incompetence, and last will and testament, chronological, 905 cases (43 drawers), 1900-1920.

Civil and Probate (Civil). Quiet titles, mortgage foreclosures, lawsuits, chronological, 851 probate court - civil cases (15 drawers), 3,720 civil cases (96 drawers), 1894-1920.

Mental Health. Lunacy cases, chronological, 125 cases (1 drawer), 1902-1920.

Miscellaneous. Executions, depositions, exhibits, judgments and transcripts (includes some probate and criminal), chronological, 720 cases (24 drawers), 1900-1920.

Election Board

None (earliest records date back to 1940s).

Sheriff

Sheriffs' Fees. 1 book, 1897-1902.

WOODWARD

Arrest Records. Chronological, 6-7 books, 1921-.

Superintendent of Schools

School Enumeration Record (Census). Name of student, date of birth, etc., by school district, chronological, 100s of books, 1912-1968.

School District Boundary Surveys. 2 books, no date.

Treasurer

Tax Rolls. Lists of real and personal property subject to taxation, shows name and address of owner, description of property, school district, state equalized value, etc., alphabetical in personal rolls, by section, township and range in real property rolls, 70 volumes, 1897 and 1900-1921.

CITIES AND TOWNS

Ada (OK 74820)

City Clerk

Council Minutes. Minutes of proceedings, includes actions taken, names of parties and dates, chronological, 6 volumes, April 8, 1901 to date.

Ordinances. Laws applicable to the city, chronological, 6 volumes, April 24, 1901 to date.

Resolutions. Formal motions starting with number 581, chronological, 1 volume, November 14, 1938 to date.

Burial Records. Names of people buried in Rosedale Cemetery, books organized by cemetery layout, 4 books, earliest date found 1905.

Cemetery Deeds. Copy of deed issued for cemetery spaces, numerical starting with number 482, 3 volumes, January 12, 1925 to date.

Altus (OK 73521)

City Clerk

Resolutions. Formal motions, chronological, 1911 to date.

Minutes. Minutes of council proceedings, chronological, 1911 to date.

Ordinances. Laws applicable to the city, chronological, 1911 to date.

Burial Record for Frazier. 1 volume.

ALVA   *CITIES AND TOWNS*

Alva (OK 73717)

City Clerk

    Ordinances and Resolutions. Index and description, chronological, 3 books, May 17, 1901 - October 5, 1920.

    Minutes. Minutes of council meetings, chronological, 3 books, February 29, 1901 - December 21, 1921.

    Cemetery. Burial records, lots and blocks, 3 books, November 6, 1898 - 1921.

Anadarko (OK 73005)

City Clerk

    None.

Antlers (OK 74523)

City Clerk

    None.

Ardmore (OK 73401)

City Clerk

    Minutes. Commission meeting minutes, chronological, 1903-.

Atoka (OK 74525)

City Clerk

    Records stored in Old City Hall (inaccessible).

CITIES AND TOWNS   BRISTOW

Bartlesville (OK 74022)

City Clerk

Original Ordinances. Various city ordinances, chronological and numerical, 11 binders (each - 4" thick), 1907 to date.

Minutes of City Commission. Minutes of city commission (council) meetings, chronological, 20 binders (each - 4" thick), May 1, 1911 to date.

Bethany (OK 73008)

City Clerk

None (no records prior to 1921). A few old photographs, newspaper clippings, etc., stored in the City Hall Museum.

Bixby (OK 74008)

City Clerk

None.

Blackwell (OK 74631)

City Clerk

Minutes of Council Meetings. Chronological, approximately 100 volumes, 1870s to date.

Ordinances. Chronological, approximately 100 volumes, 1870s to date.

Bristow (OK 74010)

City Clerk

Minutes. Proceedings of council meetings, chronological, 1 book, 1920 to date.

Broken Arrow (OK 74012)

City Clerk

Cemetery. Burial records of city owned cemetery, chronological, 1903 to date.

City Council Minutes. Minutes of proceedings, details, actions taken and all dates, chronological, no index, 1903 to date.

Ordinances. Laws enacted in town of Broken Arrow, numerical and chronological, 1903 to date.

Broken Bow (OK 74728)

City Clerk

None (no records prior to 1921).

Chandler (OK 74834)

City Clerk

City Council Minutes. Minutes of proceedings, includes details of matters discussed, actions taken, names of parties and all dates, chronological, no index, 4 volumes, June 1902-1920.

Checotah (OK 74426)

City Clerk

Minutes. Minutes of council meetings, chronological, 1900 to present.

Ordinances. Laws passed by council, chronological, 500 ordinances, 1898 to present.

Cemetery Records. Burial records and locations of cemetery lots, chronological, 1918 to present.

Resolutions. All resolutions passes by council, chronological, 1898 to present.

CITIES AND TOWNS *COLLINSVILLE*

Chickasha (OK 73018)

City Clerk

>Cemetery. Record of burials, chronological, 1925- (records prior to 1920 were destroyed in a disaster).

Choctaw (OK 73020)

City Clerk

>Records stored in attic of fire station (inaccessible).

Claremore (OK 74017)

City Clerk

>None.

Clinton (OK 73601)

City Clerk

>Minutes. Recorded motions of council actions, chronological, 2 volumes, 1909-1920.

>Ordinances. Laws enacted, chronological and numerical by ordinance number, 1 volume, 1909-1929.

>Ordinances (Codification). Chronological and numerical by ordinance number, 1 volume, 1912-.

Collinsville (OK 74021)

City Clerk

>None.

Cordell (OK 73632)

City Clerk

Minutes. Minutes of city council meetings, chronological, volume undetermined, August 10, 1909 - September 27, 1921.

Photographs. Courthouses in Cloud Chief (1898) and in Cordell (1902, 1908 and 1976).

Coweta (OK 74429)

City Clerk

None.

Cushing (OK 74023)

City Clerk

Resolutions. Resolutions passed by city commission, numbered volumes, 14 volumes, 1933 to present.

Ordinances. Ordinances passed by city commission, numbered volumes, 8 volumes, 1921 to present.

Minutes. Minutes of city commission meetings, numbered volumes, 26 volumes, 1936 to present.

Del City (OK 73115)

City Clerk

None (no records prior to 1921).

Dewey (OK 74029)

City Clerk

None (no records prior to 1920).

CITIES AND TOWNS *EL RENO*

Dickson (OK 73401)

City Clerk

None (all records were destroyed in a fire in 1984. Dickson was incorporated in the 1960s).

Drumright (OK 74030)

City Clerk

Minutes of City Commission Meetings. Record of proceedings, chronological, 1915 to date.

Ordinances. Laws applicable to the city, chronological, 1915 to date.

Duncan (OK 73633)

City Clerk

Minutes of Council Meetings. Chronological, 2-3 books, 1900-1920.

Durant (OK 74701)

City Clerk

None (no records prior to 1921).

Edmond (OK 73083)

City Clerk

Cemetery (Gracelawn). Burial and ownership records, burial cards (alphabetical), ownership (legal description), index cards and 2 volumes, 1890 to date.

El Reno (OK 73036)

Deputy City Clerk

Fire Department. Daily log book, chronological, 3 notebooks, 1904-1920.

EL RENO *CITIES AND TOWNS*

Tax Sale Records (county). Chronological, 65 volumes, 1905-1920.

Justice Dockets (county). Chronological, 100 volumes, 1890-1920.

Commissioner Records (county). Chronological, 11 volumes, 1890-1920.

Miscellaneous (county). Medical registrations, indictments, government entry records, field notes, voters' registrations, elections and notaries, chronological, 15 volumes, 1892-1920.

Cemetery Ledgers (city). Grave locations in "potters field", negro cemeteries and other cemeteries, chronological, 10 volumes, 1890-1920.

Paving Tax Records (city). Chronological, 3 volumes, 1909-1920.

Bonds Record Book (city). Sewer, water and park improvements, etc., chronological, 3 volumes, 1895-1920.

Sewer and Sidewalk Warrants Record (city). Chronological, 1 volume, 1914-1920.

Minutes. Proceedings of city council meetings, chronological, 9 volumes, 1890-1920.

Ordinance Records (city). Chronological, 5 volumes, 1893-1920.

Note: Additional records stored in the El Reno Carnegie Library and the El Reno Fire Department, El Reno, OK.

Elk City (OK 73644)

City Clerk

City Commission Minutes. Minutes of meetings, actions taken, names of parties, and formation of committees, chronological, 2 volumes, 1923 to date.

Ordinance Book. Contains all ordinances, resolutions and laws, chronological, 1 volume, 1907-1920.

CITIES AND TOWNS *ENID*

Enid (OK 73701)

City Clerk

Council Minutes. Council minutes of mayor and board of commissioners after Enid was declared a "city of the first class" by governor on October 7, 1893, chronological, books 1 through 9, November 10, 1893 - December 20, 1920.

Official Bond Register. Water and sewer bond issues and city funding, chronological, book number 1, 1894-1908.

Gross Tax Certification Record. Record of bonds as issued for sanitary sewer, storm sewer, public utilities, water works and sewage disposal, chronological, book number 1, 1908-1920.

Municipal Bond Register. Water and sewer bond issues, chronological, book number 2, 1900-1919.

Municipal Bond Register. General obligation issue and water works, chronological, book number 3, 1919.

Financial Ledger. List of all collections and expenditures, chronological, 1900-1917.

Ordinances. Actual ordinance as passed and approved by the mayor and board of commissioners, chronological, ordinance numbers 1 through 1146, 1893-1920.

Ordinance Record. Recordation of ordinances, numerical by ordinance number and date passed, books 1 through 6, ordinance numbers 1 through 1146, 1893-1920.

Contract Record. Contracts and agreements as entered into with contractors and other diversified entities, alphabetical by contractor and entity, book numbers 1 and 2, 1910-1926.

Clerks' Warrant Register. A listing of claims as paid by city, departmentally and then by claim number, book numbers 1 and 2, 1894 - December 30, 1920.

Treasurers' Warrant Register. A listing of warrants as paid on approval of the mayor and board of commissioners, chronological and numerical by warrant number, books 1 and 2, 1894 - December 30, 1920.

ENID *CITIES AND TOWNS*

Paving Assessment Record. Paving assessments for street improvements, chronological by addition and legal description, series A, books 1 through 50, 1894-1920.

Financial Ledger. Listing of receipts and expenditures, departmentally and then by claim number, 1918-1919.

Easements. Instruments conveying easements to city of Enid, numerical by assigned number and alphabetical, December 1909 - January 1918.

Deeds. Instruments conveying property to city of Enid, by assigned number in order as accepted, numbers 1 through 93, June 11, 1894 - October 17, 1920.

Sidewalk Assessments. Special sidewalk assessment districts, by legal description, 1909-1921.

Municipal Bond Register. General obligation bond issue for funding water, sewage disposal, city hall and parks, chronological, book number 1, 1909-1911.

Municipal Bond Register. General obligation bond issue for water and city hall, chronological, book number 4, 1919-1920.

Note: Some records are stored in the Old City Hall (vacated by the office of the City Clerk in 1976.)

Eufaula (OK 74432)

City Clerk

None (some records are stored in the Eufaula Public Library, Eufaula, OK).

Fairview (OK 73737)

City Clerk

Minutes. Proceedings of council meetings, chronological, 2-3 volumes, 1903-1920.

Cemetery Record. Alphabetical, several volumes, 1903-1920.

Resolutions. Chronological, 1 volume, 1903-1920.

Frederick (OK 73542)

City Clerk

City Council Minutes. Minutes of proceedings include details of matters discussed, actions taken, names of parties involved, chronological, 2 volumes, April 1907 - December 1920.

Ordinances. Handwritten ordinances governing Frederick, chronological, one volume, 1907-1912.

Newspapers. Newspapers on microfilm (Frederick Leader), 1904-1920.

Note: Additional records stored in the Frederick Public Library, Frederick, OK.

Grove (OK 74344)

City Clerk

Minutes. Proceedings of council meetings, chronological, 8-10 volumes, 1912 to date (minutes as early as 1867 kept in storage).

Ordinances. Chronological, 8-10 volumes, 1867 to date.

Guthrie (OK 73044)

City Clerk

Guthrie City Records Collection - East Guthrie. Quit Claim deeds, court dockets, record of ordinances, record of mayors' certificates, transfer record, justices' civil docket, certificate record, record (city council minutes), register of claims and warrants, and indexes, "Inventory of Guthrie Records Collection" (finding aid), 19 volumes, 1889-1891.

Guthrie City Records Collection - Capital Hill. Treasurers' record, record of deeds and sale of lots, register of lot holders, treasurers' book, and register of deeds, "Inventory of Guthrie Records Collection" (finding aid), 6 volumes, 1889-1891.

Guthrie City Records Collection - Guthrie Proper. Arbitration court record, warranty certificates issued, list of lot claimants and improvements, cash book, record of ordinances, cash (building records and permits), proceedings of

GUTHRIE *CITIES AND TOWNS*

council, record of affidavits of claimants, "Inventory of Guthrie Records Collections" (finding aid), 9 volumes, 1889-1890.

Guthrie City Records Collection - City of Guthrie. City council minutes (13 volumes, 1890-1923), record of ordinances (8 volumes, 1890-1921), city treasurer and city clerk (claim, warrant and cash books, 30 volumes, 1889-1928), Guthrie claims commission (1 volume, 1891), water department (water register, list of water taps, 15 volumes, 1893-1949), "Inventory of Guthrie Records Collections" (finding aid), 15 volumes, 1889-1949.

Guthrie City Records Collection - City of Guthrie (continued). Fire department (day book, minutes of firemen relief and pension fund board, 4 volumes, 1892-1923), park board (register, 2 volumes, 1912-1914), occupational tax (record, 2 volumes, 1889-1921), poll tax (2 volumes, 1895-1923), "Inventory of Guthrie City Records Collection" (finding aid), 10 volumes, 1889-1923.

Guthrie City Records Collection - City of Guthrie (continued). Special tax roll, Logan County (1 volume, 1895), automobile and motorcycle registration (1 volume, 1911-1916), saloon license record (1 volume, 1892-1897), dog register (1 volume, 1912-1929), marshals' record (1 volume, no date), "Inventory of Guthrie City Records Collection" (finding aid), 5 volumes, 1892-1929.

Guthrie City Records Collection - City of Guthrie (continued). Jail calendar (4 volumes, 1900-1927), police judges' docket (30 volumes, 1890-1920), reward and wanted notices (1 volume, 1905-1907), Guthrie board of education (minutes, school attendance, 5 volumes, 1889-1911), "Inventory of Guthrie Records Collection" (finding aid), 40 volumes, 1889-1927.

Guthrie City Records Collection - City of Guthrie (continued). Cemetery record (record of internments, financial records of minutes, 9 volumes, 1890-1936), voter registration journal (1 volume, 1889-1908), "Inventory of Guthrie Records Collection" (finding aid), 10 volumes, 1889-1936.

Note: Microfilm of the Guthrie City Records Collection is stored in the Guthrie Public Library, Guthrie, OK.

Logan County Historical Society, Guthrie, OK

County Assessments. Tax assessments on both real and personal property, chronological, approximately 50 volumes, 1889-1930s.

City Records. Municipal minutes, sheriffs' records, court records and water department records, microfilm (stored in the Guthrie Public Library), 1889-1910.

CITIES AND TOWNS *HENRYETTA*

Newspapers. Microfilm of Daily Oklahoma State Capitol and Oklahoma State Capitol (stored in the State Capitol Publishing Museum, Guthrie, OK), 1889-1910.

Building Permits. Numerical by permit number, 1 volume (stored in the Guthrie Public Library), 1901-1948.

City Directories (stored in the Oklahoma Territorial Museum, Guthrie, OK). Names and addresses, alphabetical, 1889-1940s.

Early Photographs of Guthrie (stored in the Bozarth Studios, Guthrie, OK). Primarily commercial photographs, 100s of prints, 1889-1930.

Guymon (OK 73942)

City Clerk

City Council Minutes. Minutes of proceedings, chronological, approximately 3 books, ca. 1907 to date.

Cemetery Records. Ownership and burial (names), alphabetical, 2 cemetery books from 1 funeral director, ca. 1907 to date.

Healdton (OK 73438)

City Clerk

None.

Henryetta (OK 74437)

City Clerk

Cemetery Record. 10,000 graves, chronological and alphabetical, 1911-1920.

Minutes. Proceedings of council meetings, chronological, 20 volumes, 1911-1920.

Resolutions. Chronological, 4 volumes, 1911-1920.

Ordinances. Chronological, 4 volumes, 1911-1920.

HOBART   CITIES AND TOWNS

Hobart (OK 73651)

City Clerk

   City Council Minutes. Minutes of proceedings, actions taken, members present, etc., chronological, 5 volumes, 1902 to date.

Holdenville (OK 74848)

City Clerk

   Cemetery Deeds and Cemetery Spaces. Lists owner of lots and how many lots purchased, chronological, 1908 to date.

   Minutes. Minutes of meetings of the City Council of Holdenville and the Holdenville Public Works Authority, chronological, 1908 to date.

   Note: Additional records are stored at the Hughes County Historical Society.

Hollis (OK 73550)

City Clerk

   No records prior to 1929, when Hollis was established.

Idabel (OK 74745)

City Clerk

   Ordinances. Ordinance numbers 1 through 162, chronological and indexed, 1 volume, 1906-1921.

Jenks (OK 74037)

City Clerk

   Court Dates. Docket book, chronological, one volume, 1932-1934.

   Minutes. Minute book, chronological, one volume, 1920-1930.

CITIES AND TOWNS *MCALESTER*

Kingfisher (OK 73750)

City Clerk

None.

Lawton (OK 73501)

City Clerk

City Council Minutes of Proceedings. Minutes of city business, chronological, indexed alphabetically, 3 books, September 12, 1910 - January 20, 1921.

City Ordinances. Ordinances adopted by the city council, chronological, indexed alphabetically, 3 books, October 30, 1901 - January 2, 1937.

Note: Additional records stored in the Museum of the Great Plains and the Lawton Public Library, Lawton, OK.

Lone Grove (OK 73443)

City Clerk

None.

McAlester (OK 74501)

City Clerk

City Council Minutes. Minutes of proceedings include details of matters discussed, actions taken, names of parties and all dates, chronological and index since 1979, several volumes, 1900 to date.

City Ordinances. Actions pertaining to city codes, chronological and indexed, several volumes, 1900 to date.

Resolutions. Actions pertaining to city activities, chronological and indexed, several folders, dates undetermined.

McLoud (OK 74851)

City Clerk

Cemetery Deed Record. Filed instrument, 1 item (copy), September 4, 1901.

County Commissioners' Meeting Minutes. Proceedings of meeting of county commissioners in which the town of McLoud was declared an incorporated town, 1 item, July 1896.

Madill (OK 73446)

City Clerk

None.

Mangum (OK 73554)

City Clerk

None (no records prior to 1921).

Marlow (OK 73055)

City Clerk

Minutes. City council meetings (handwritten), chronological, 2 books, 1908-1921.

Cemetery Records. Chronological, alphabetical, 1 book, 1908-1921.

Ordinances. Chronological, 1 book, 1908-1921.

Miami (OK 74354)

City Clerk

City Council Minutes. Chronological, 6 volumes, 1899-1926.

Ordinance Book. Ordinances, chronological, 4 volumes, 1895-1921.

CITIES AND TOWNS *MUSKOGEE*

Midwest City (OK 73140)

City Clerk

No records prior to 1943, when Midwest City was incorporated.

Moore (OK 73160)

City Clerk

Agendas and Minutes. Listing of agenda items and recorded minutes, chronological, 1892 to date.

Ordinances. Full recorded ordinance, by number and year, July 1964 to date.

Resolutions. Full recorded resolution, by number and year, 1973 to date.

Cemetery Files. Files concerning Moore Cemetery since 1919, and Smith Cemetery since 1950.

Utility Records. Contracts, payment stubs, billings, final and transfer registers, and posting revenues registers, volume and dates undetermined.

Muskogee (OK 74401)

City Clerk

Council Minutes. Minutes of proceedings, actions taken and names of parties, chronological, some indexing, 20 volumes, 1898-1920.

Ordinance Books. Ordinances adopted by council, some legal publications included, and dates adopted, chronological, 6 volumes, 1898-1920.

Greenhill Cemetery Deed Books. Date of death, name, funeral home involved, cause of death, age at death, 3 volumes, 1898-1920.

Greenhill Cemetery Deeds. Copies of original deeds signed by mayor and city clerk, location of property, cost and owner of property, alphabetical, 1 volume, 1904-1920.

MUSKOGEE *CITIES AND TOWNS*

City Charter (copy). Provided for form of government, method of elections, terms of governing board, and rules for city (Muskogee's original charter stored in the Oklahoma Department of Libraries, State Archives Division, Oklahoma City, OK), 1 item, 1922.

Sanitary Sewer Districts. 1 volume, 1916-1920.

Mustang (OK 73064)

City Clerk

None.

Newcastle (OK 73065)

City Clerk

None (no records prior to 1920).

Nichols Hills (OK 73116)

City Clerk

None.

Noble (OK 73068)

City Hall

Town Council Minutes. Record of town council meetings, chronological, 1938 to present.

Ordinances/Proclamations. Chronological, 1908 to present.

Norman (OK 73070)

City Clerk

City Council Minutes. Minutes of proceedings, includes details of matters discussed, actions taken, names of parties and all dates, chronological, no index,

CITIES AND TOWNS *OKLAHOMA CITY*

6 volumes, June 4, 1891 - 1920.

City of Norman Ordinances. Ordinances passed by city council, names of signers and all dates, numerical by ordinance number, 2 volumes, April 10, 1902 - 1920.

Nowata (OK 74048)

City Clerk

Minutes. City council meetings and other city business meetings, chronological, several volumes, 1909 to date.

Ordinances. City ordinances, numerical, several volumes, 1910 to date.

Cemetery Books. Recording of name, lot, block space and dates, alphabetical, several books, ca. 1905 to date.

Note: Additional records stored in the Benjamin Funeral Home and the Nowata County Historical Society, Nowata, OK.

Okemah (OK 74859)

City Clerk

None.

Oklahoma City (OK 73102)

City Clerk

City Council Minutes. Minutes of council proceedings, details of discussions, actions taken, dates and names of parties, chronological and indexed, 23 volumes, 1890-1920.

Ordinances. Laws and regulations approved by mayor and council, chronological and indexed, 2,264 items, 1890-1920.

Contracts. Construction jobs and material items purchased, chronological and indexed, 134 items, 1893-1920.

OKLAHOMA CITY *CITIES AND TOWNS*

Deed. Deed to old city dump on east Reno, chronological and indexed, 1 item, 1902.

Special Assessments. Tax levied on all property for street grading, sidewalks, weeds, filling lots, curbs, guttering, street sprinklers and sanitary sewers, chronological and indexed, 760 items, 1891-1920.

Metropolitan Library System

Building Ordinance of Oklahoma City, Oklahoma in Force November 24, 1909. Building codes, chronological, 1 volume, 1909.

Charter and Revised General Ordinances. Miscellaneous information regarding building codes and other regulations, chronological, 2 volumes, 1913-1915.

Annual Financial Statement, Oklahoma City. Financial records, some photographs of public buildings, business establishments and city officials, brief reports of city offices, chronological, 1 volume, 1911-1915.

Course of Study and Superintendents' Reports of the Oklahoma City Public Schools. Outline of the curriculum taught, financial statements, and small pictures of each school in the Oklahoma City public school system, chronological, 1 volume, 1906-1909.

Report to the Mayor and Board of Commissioners of Oklahoma City on an Improved Water Supply for the City. Water supply deficiencies, recommendations for improvements from the board of engineers, maps, chronological, 1 volume, 1913.

Report on an Improved Water Supply for the City of Oklahoma City, Oklahoma. Recommendations to Dan V. Lachey, mayor, and the city council for an improved water supply, maps, tables, geological data pertaining to the system in use, correspondence and newspaper clippings concerning the project, chronological, 1 volume, 1911-1919.

Okmulgee (OK 74447)

City Clerk

Ordinances. Criminal and general ordinances, some handwritten (original) and others retyped by the Works Progress Administration, chronological, 4 volumes, 1901-1920.

CITIES AND TOWNS   PERRY

Fireman Annual Report. Names of fire chiefs, city clerks, firemen and terminated firemen, chronological, 1 volume, 1915-1920.

Owasso (OK 74055)

City Clerk

None (no records prior to 1933).

Pauls Valley (OK 73035)

City Clerk

None.

Pawhuska (OK 74056)

City Clerk

Cemetery. Burials, alphabetical, 1 volume, 1888-1920.

Minutes of City Council Meetings. Minutes, chronological, 3 volumes, 1906-1920.

Perry (OK 73077)

City Clerk

Ordinances. Chronological, numbers 1 through 336, volume number 1, October 30, 1893 - November 12, 1900.

Ordinances. Chronological, numbers 337 through 698, volume B, November 19, 1900 - December 3, 1912.

Ordinances. Chronological, numbers 699 through 1070, volume C, January 17, 1913 - February 16, 1931.

Cash Book. Volume number 1, November 10, 1893 - April 9, 1897.

Council Minutes. Cherokee Strip opened September 16, 1893, chronological, volume number 1, October 28, 1893 - April 9, 1897.

PERRY *CITIES AND TOWNS*

Council Minutes. Chronological, volume B, April 12, 1897 - December 6, 1904.

Council Minutes. Chronological and alphabetical, volume C, January 13, 1905 - February 16, 1909.

Council Minutes. Chronological, volume D, October 19, 1909 - August 27, 1919.

Council Minutes. Chronological, volume E, August 27, 1919 - July 10, 1928.

Council Minutes. Chronological, volume F, July 10, 1928 - May 1, 1931.

Pocola (OK 74902)

City Clerk

None (no records prior to 1963).

Ponca City (OK 74601)

City Clerk

City Ordinances. Ordinances setting municipal laws and regulations, dated as approved, and codified into city code book, chronological, no index, 6 volumes, 1894-1920.

City Resolutions. Appointment of city officials, establishment of street improvement districts, issuance of street improvement bonds, determination of material to be used for street improvements, authorization of bid advertisements, approval of engineers' estimates and award of contracts to construct streets, chronological, no index, 1 volume, 1920-1927.

City Council Minutes. Minutes of proceedings include details of items discussed, actions taken, manner of vote by council members, names of persons in attendance, all dates of agreements approved, dates of meetings and minute approval dates, chronological, no index, 4 volumes, 1905-1926.

CITIES AND TOWNS *SAND SPRINGS*

Poteau (OK 74953)

City Clerk

> City Council Minutes. Minutes of proceedings, chronological, 4 volumes, 1889-1932.

Pryor (OK 74361)

City Clerk

> Minutes. 2 volumes, July 5, 1906 and 1912-1931.
>
> Oath of Office Book. 1 volume, 1911-1945.
>
> Cemetery Records. Volume and dates undetermined.

Purcell (OK 73080)

City Clerk

> Minutes. Minutes of city commission meetings, chronological, 1898 to date.

Sallisaw (OK 74955)

City Clerk

> City Council Minutes. Record of business transacted, action taken, members present, etc., chronological, no index, one volume, April 5, 1911 - 1923.

Sand Springs (OK 74063)

City Clerk

> Ordinances. Laws of the city of Sand Springs, chronological, 1 volume, 1912-1921.

Sapulpa (OK 74066)

City Clerk

Ordinances. Numerical, 1902 to date.

Resolutions. Numerical, 1909 to date.

City Council Minutes. Minutes of proceedings, actions taken, names of parties and all dates, chronological, 1922 to date.

Cemetery Records. Name of deceased, date of burial, location of burial, cause of death, age of deceased, owner of burial space, chronological and alphabetical, 1895 to date.

Court Docket Books. Names of persons fined, amounts of fines, verdicts, chronological, ca. 1895 to date.

Sayre (OK 73662)

City Clerk

Record of Council Proceedings. Minutes of council meetings (includes first meeting held in Sayre, Oklahoma Territory for purpose of incorporation of the town), chronological, 1 volume, 1903-1910.

Record of Council Proceedings. Minutes of council meetings, chronological, 1 volume, 1910-1923.

Seminole (OK 74868)

City Clerk

The city of Seminole was declared in 1927. This office has no records prior to that date.

Shawnee (OK 74801)

City Clerk

Charter. Document creating a public or private corporation, includes laws and ordinances, 1 volume, adopted 1908, amended 1930.

CITIES AND TOWNS *SPENCER*

Ordinances. Statutes and regulations enacted by city government, chronological, 217 items (4 volumes), July 1894 - April 1923.

City Commission Minutes. Minutes of proceedings, includes details of matters discussed, actions taken, names of parties and all dates, chronological (indexed), December 1894 - August 1924.

Petition to Incorporate. Petition includes legal description of territory, signatures of applicants voting for the petition, and exact date of incorporation, 1 document, October 1893.

Correspondence Pertaining to the Carnegie Library. Grants issued for construction of the Carnegie Library, and requirements for public libraries by Oklahoma Territory, 1 item, 1903-1928.

Note: Additional records stored in the Pottawatomie County Courthouse and the Shawnee Public Library, Shawnee, OK.

Skiatook (OK 74070)

City Clerk

Minutes. Minutes of the meetings of the board of trustees, chronological, 2 books, 1908-1921.

Ordinances. Ordinances of the town of Skiatook, chronological, 2 books, 1908-1921.

Court Records. Court dockets and dispensation of cases, Skiatook Municipal Court, chronological, 9 books, 1907-1921.

Claims/Warrant Register. Warrant register of all claims paid by town of Skiatook, chronological, 2 books, 1912-1921.

Spencer (OK 73084)

City Clerk

None (no records prior to 1948. The town of Spencer was incorporated in 1949 and became a city in 1970).

STILLWATER *CITIES AND TOWNS*

Stillwater (OK 74076)

Finance Department

Record of Formation of Township. Formation of township before the Oklahoma land run, chronological, 1 volume, 1888 - April 1889.

Minutes. Records of town meetings, chronological, 6 volumes, April 1891 - December 1921.

Ordinances. Record of ordinances governing the city of Stillwater, chronological, 3 volumes, December 1909 - April 1933.

Pay Records of Special Assessments. Pay records for paving districts, numbers 1 through 20, chronological, 1 volume, 1914-1924.

Bond Register. Bonds for street improvements, chronological, 1 volume, August 1892 - June 1924.

Note: Additional records stored in the Sherrar Museum, Stillwater, OK.

Stroud (OK 74079)

City Clerk

None (no records prior to 1921).

Tahlequah (OK 74464)

City Hall

Minutes of Town Council. Handwritten minutes of council meetings, chronological, 3 bound books, 1894-1923.

Ordinance Books. Handwritten ordinances of city of Tahlequah, chronological, 2 bound books, 1908-1911.

Police Judge Reports. Monthly reports of cases tried, chronological, approximately 30 small books, 1910 to date.

Financial Ledger Books. Sanitary sewer warrants issued, collection distributions, claims and vouchers, and treasurers' reports, chronological, 1911 to date.

CITIES AND TOWNS *TISHOMINGO*

Burial Ledger and Books. Records of burial and cemetery plat book, chronological, ledger and books, 1906 to date.

Miscellaneous Material. Street improvement projects, Carnegie Library information, resolutions, requests for job positions, applications, permits, licenses, etc., volume undetermined, early 1900s.

Tecumseh (OK 74873)

City Clerk

Minutes. Minute records of the city of Tecumseh, chronological, 1 volume, October 5, 1914 - May 7, 1923.

Accountant Record. County minutes when Tecumseh was the county seat, 1 volume, 1904-1905.

Tonkawa (OK 74653)

City Clerk

Minutes. Minutes of council meetings, chronological, 1904 to date.

Ordinances. Laws, arranged numerically, 7 volumes, 1902 to date.

The Village (OK 73120)

City Clerk

None (The Village was incorporated as a town in 1950).

Tishomingo (OK 73460)

City Clerk

None.

Tulsa (OK 74103)

Auditor

Minutes of Commission Meetings. Minutes of city government meetings, chronological, 15 volumes, 1906-1920.

Fireman's Pension Board. Minutes, chronological, 1 volume, 1913-1935.

Contracts. Copies of all contracts entered into by the city, chronological, 3 linear feet, 1906-1920.

Easements. Copies of land easements, chronological, 4 file drawers, 1914-1920.

Resolutions. Resolutions passed by the city, chronological, 1 file box, 1908-1940.

Ordinances. City ordinances, chronological, 5 file boxes, 1900-1920.

Municipal Court Clerk

Criminal Dockets. Date of arrest, criminal charge, disposition, fine amount, court costs and fees, defendant's name, judge's name, mayor's name, and fine payment information, chronological, 29 microfilm cartridges, 1899-1921.

Note: Additional records stored in the Tulsa County Historical Society, Tulsa, OK.

Tuttle (OK 73089)

City Clerk

Ordinances and Council Minutes. Chronological, 1 volume, 1906-1971.

Council Minutes. Chronological, 1 volume, 1933-1949.

Ordinances and Resolutions. Chronological, 2 volumes, 1944 to date.

Cemetery Deeds. Chronological, alphabetical, 25 books, 1909 to date.

Cemetery Ledger. Chronological, alphabetical, 1 volume, 1909 to date.

Cemetery Minutes. Chronological, alphabetical, 1 volume, 1987 to date.

CITIES AND TOWNS   *WEATHERFORD*

Vinita (OK 74301)

City Clerk

    City Council Meetings. Minutes of proceedings, chronological, 1889 to date.

    City Ordinances. Ordinances making city policies, chronological, 1889 to date.

    Cemetery. Deed ownership, burials, chronological, 1907 to date.

Wagoner (OK 74467)

City Clerk

    Cemetery. Burial permits and certificates of purchase, alphabetical, index, 3 volumes, 1906 to date.

Warr Acres (OK 73122)

City Clerk

    None (Warr Acres did not exist in 1920. The area was stop fourteen on the interurban to El Reno).

Watonga (OK 73772)

City Clerk

    Minutes of Council Meetings. Business transacted by city, chronological, 3 volumes, 1901-1920.

Weatherford (OK 73096)

City Clerk

    Council Minutes. Minutes of proceedings, chronological, no index, 2 volumes, 1901-1920.

WEWOKA

Wewoka (OK 74884)

City Clerk/Treasurer

Cemetery Record. Cemetery burial records, cemetery committee minutes and check register, chronological, partial index, 2 volumes, 1911-1923.

Warrant Register. Checks issued by name and purpose, chronological, 1 volume, 1915-1944.

Note: Additional records stored in the Seminole Nation Museum, Wewoka, OK.

Wilburton (OK 74578)

City Clerk

None.

Woodward (OK 73801)

City Clerk

Board of Trustees Minutes, Ordinances and Resolutions. Minutes of proceedings, includes details of matters discussed, motions made, actions taken, names of parties and dates, ordinances and resolutions for the town of Woodward, Oklahoma Territory, chronological, index to ordinances, 3 volumes, 1901-1906.

City Council Minutes. Minutes of proceedings, includes details of matters discussed, motions made, actions taken, names of parties and dates, chronological, no index, 2 volumes, 1906-1922.

City Ordinances (passed after statehood). Ordinances, one proclamation, subject matter, signatures of mayors and city clerks, dates passed, certifications of passage date and publication by the city clerk, chronological, index, 1 volume, 1907-1928.

Cemetery Records. Name of purchaser, cost, date deed was issued, lot, block, grave information and information on deceased, by lot, block and grave number, alphabetical index, 7 ledgers, 1907- (these ledgers have been transferred to current cemetery ledgers).

CITIES AND TOWNS *YUKON*

City Bond Registers. Type of bond, bond number, date, amount, purpose, rate of interest and coupon information, bonds for water works, sewer, water extension, refunding, electric light, park funds, city hall and funding, chronological, index, 2 volumes, 1906-1923.

Deeds and Abstracts of Title. Various deeds and abstracts of title wherein land was given to the city of Woodward, volume undetermined, 1902-1920.

Yukon (OK 73085)

City Clerk

City Council Minutes. Minutes of matters briefly discussed, actions taken and names of parties (some illegible), no index, 2 volumes, 1901-1923.

GENERAL REPOSITORIES

Oklahoma Department of Libraries, State Archives Division (Oklahoma City, OK 73105)

Minutes of the Boards of County Commissioners. Transcripts of original minutes of meetings of boards of county commissioners for forty-seven Oklahoma counties, includes information about road construction, purchase of supplies and equipment, formation of towns and villages, contract awards, jail construction and local election results, arranged by county, 30 linear feet, 1886-1939.

Oklahoma Department of Libraries, State Records Center (Oklahoma City, OK 73105)

Cleveland County

Marriage Licenses. 50 cubic feet, 1890-1944.

Divorce Cases. 30 cubic feet, 1932-1955.

District Civil Cases. 125 cubic feet, 1896-1955.

County Civil Cases. 30 cubic feet, 1890-1944.

Note: The State Records Center also has security copy microfilm of some county records. The master negatives cannot be used for reference searches and many of the records are listed as confidential. Researchers interested in examining microfilm copies of county records should contact the appropriate county.

Oklahoma Historical Society, Archives and Manuscripts Division (Oklahoma City, OK 73105)

Comanche County

Journal of the District Court. 4 volumes, 1901-1907.

Sheriffs' Fee. 5 volumes, 1903-1910.

Witness. 1 volume, 1905-1910.

Docket, Appearance (Civil). 1 volume, 1903-1907.

Docket, Execution. 1 volume, 1901-1908.

Census: Agriculture and Other Statistics (City of Lawton). 1 volume, 1905.

Indictment Record (United States). 1 volume, 1902-1907.

Sheriffs' Criminal Docket (Book Numbers 2, 4 and 6). 3 volumes, 1907-1915.

Sheriffs' Criminal Fee. 1 volume, 1903-1905.

Equity. 1 volume, ca. 1904.

Greer County

Docket (Civil), Appearance. 1 volume, 1891-1898.

Docket (Civil), Justices, Precinct Number 1. 1 volume, 1886-1890.

Docket (Civil), Justices, Precinct Number 2. 1 volume, 1891-1895.

Docket (Civil), Motion. 1 volume, 1892-1895.

Execution Docket, Index, District Court. 1 volume, no date.

Garnishment, Affidavit and Bond. 1 affidavit, 1890.

Minutes, Index, District Court. 1 volume, no date.

Subpoenas (Civil). 1 volume, 1893-1895.

Animals and Hides, Record of Inspection. 1 volume, 1887-1893.

Butchers' Record. 1 volume, 1889-1893.

Commissioners' Court, Docket. 1 volume, 1890-1891.

Commissioners' Court, Minutes, Transcribed. 1 volume, 1890.

Deed of Trust. 1 volume, 1886-1889.

GENERAL REPOSITORIES *OKLAHOMA HISTORICAL SOCIETY*

Deeds, General Index. 1 volume, 1886-1890.

Deputations, Record. 1 volume, 1894-1896.

Estrays, Record. 1 volume, 1887-1895.

Liquor Licenses. 1 certificate, 24 receipt stubs, 1896-1900.

Mark and Brand Record. 1 volume, 1888-1891.

Notarial Bond. 1 volume, 1891-1895.

Occupation License. 2 receipt stubs, 1 certificate, 1891.

Official Bonds, Records. 3 volumes, 1886-1895.

Road Minutes. 1 volume, 1891-1896.

Superintendents' School Record. 1 volume, 1892-1893.

Surveyors' Field Notes. 1 volume, 1888-1892.

County Funds Balances. 1 volume, 1896-1898.

Finance Ledger. 1 volume, 1886-1893.

Treasurers' Receipts. 1 volume, 1886-1894.

Treasurers' School Account Register. 1 volume, 1891-1892.

Warning of Tax Delinquency. 1 postcard, 1896.

Docket (Criminal), Judges. 2 volumes, 1895-1898.

Docket (Criminal), Justices, Precinct Number 1. 1 volume, 1886-1891.

Docket (Criminal), Motion, County Court. 1 volume, 1892-1897.

Docket (Criminal), Motion, District Court. 1 volume, 1888-1895.

Foreign Sheriffs' Accounts, Minutes. 1 volume, 1894-1895.

Grand Jury, Minutes. 1 volume, 1891-1894.

Jail Calendar. 1 volume, 1898-1905.

Minutes, Sheriffs' Foreign, County Attorney, District Attorney Accounts. 1 volume, 1891-1896.

Prisoners, Register. 1 volume, 1888-1917.

Scire Facias Docket. 1 volume, 1888-1896.

Scire Facias Minutes, District Court. 1 volume, 1891-1896.

Sheriffs' Accounts, Minutes. 1 volume, 1890-1896.

Subpoenas (Criminal Cases). 1 volume, 1893-1895.

Witness Accounts, Minutes. 1 volume, 1889-1896.

Witness Attachments (Criminal Cases). 79 receipt stubs, 1 attachment form, 1893-1896.

Attorneys' Orders. 1 page, 1894.

Attorneys' Receipt for Papers. 1 volume, 1894-1897.

Clerks' File Docket, County Court. 1 volume, 1887-1896.

Clerks' File Docket, District Court. 1 volume, 1886-1896.

Jurors' Certificates. 8 certificates, 58 receipt stubs, 1894-1896.

Motion Docket and Scire Facias Docket. 1 volume, 1890.

Superintendents' School Record. 1 volume, 1890-1895.

Johnston County

Claims and Fees Notebook. 1908-1911.

Dockets. 1916-1936.

Minutes, Court Clerks' Notebooks. 1907-1917.

Miscellaneous Matters for Journal Entry. 1916-1920.

Sheriffs' Day Book. 1 volume, 1921-1922.

Witness Records, Certificates of Attendance. 1 booklet, 1916-1920.

GENERAL REPOSITORIES   *OKLAHOMA HISTORICAL SOCIETY*

Case Packets. 1908-1937.

Claims Against the County. 1909-1924.

County Clerks' Quarterly Reports (Fees Collected). 1907-1910.

County Commissioners, Records. 1908-1936.

Insanity Case Packets. 1907-1938.

Official Appointments. 1908-1932.

Public Health and Safety Orders. 1916-1919.

Case Packets. 1907-1941.

Jurors, Records, Grand Jury Minutes. 2 notebooks, 1909-1910.

Jurors, Records, Lists of Names of Jurors. 1915-1920.

Jurors, Records, Orders for Petit Juries. 1916-1921.

Jurors, Records, Venire for Petit Juries. 1915-1921.

Pardon and Parole Correspondence. 1911-1930.

Receipts for Commitments to State Institutions of Correction. 1909-1935.

Administrators and Executors, Records. 1908 and 1917-1940.

Guardians, Records. 1913-1920.

Annual Returns, Public Utilities. 1908-1911 and 1919-1921.

Annual Statements, Banks. 1908-1911.

Assessment Lists, Banks and Other Corporations. 1910-1911 and 1917-1921.

Assessment Lists, Personal and Real Property. 1911.

Assessments, Public Service Corporations. 1908.

Assessments, Railroad Property. 1908-1909.

Certificates of Assessment, Railroad Property. 1908-1911 and 1919-1921.

OKLAHOMA HISTORICAL SOCIETY   GENERAL REPOSITORIES

   Land Plats. ca. 1917.

   Right-Of-Way, Railroad. 1909.

   County Financial Statements. 1907-1908.

   Quarterly Reports. 1908-1909.

   Township Financial Statements and Reports. 1911-1913 and 1921.

Kiowa County

   Bond. 1 volume, 1905-1907.

   Claims Allowed. 1 volume, 1901-1910.

   Dockets, Justice (Hobart). 4 volumes, 1902-1911.

   Fees Charged and Received by Probate Judge. 1 volume, 1901-1909.

   Fees Received (and apportioned), Account ("Cash Book 1"). 1 volume, 1902-1914.

   Sheriffs' Process. 1 volume, 1917-1922.

   Civil Actions in Equity, or at Law. 1 volume, 1904-1906.

   Attorneys, Roster. 1 volume, 1894-1910.

   Liquor Dealers Bond. 1 volume, 1901-1904.

   Liquor License Fee. 11 sheets, 1901-1903.

   Notarial. 1 volume, 1901-1917.

   Notary Commission. 1 volume, 1902-1917.

   Official Bond. 1 volume, 1901-1916.

   Court Proceedings. 1 volume, 1905-1907.

   Guardians. 1 volume, 1905-1910.

   Guardians' Report. 1 volume, 1903-1913.

GENERAL REPOSITORIES   *OKLAHOMA HISTORICAL SOCIETY*

Inventory and Appraisement. 1 volume, 1903-1912.

Assessment Rolls, Cooperton Township. 4 volumes, 1903-1907.

Assessment Rolls, Dill Township. 4 volumes, 1903-1905.

Assessment Rolls, Harrison Township. 5 volumes, 1902-1906.

Assessment Rolls, Hobart City. 3 volumes, 1903-1904 and 1907.

Assessment Rolls, Hobart Township. 6 volumes, 1903-1906.

Assessment Rolls, Hunter Township. 4 volumes, 1903-1906.

Assessment Rolls, Lone Wolf City. 1 volume, 1902.

Assessment Rolls, Mount Park Township. 5 volumes, 1903-1907.

Assessment Rolls, Mountain View Township. 6 volumes, 1903-1907.

Assessment Rolls, Otter Creek Township. 5 volumes, 1902-1907.

Land and Lots, Hobart Township. 1 volume, 1911-1914.

Mining District Deed (A), Otter Creek Township. 1 volume, 1901-1907.

Mining Operations, Otter Creek Township. 1 volume, 1901-1904.

Tax, Inheritance. 1 volume, 1911-1929.

Tax Rolls, Municipalities. 12 volumes, 1902-1907.

Tax Rolls, Townships. 6 volumes, 1903-1907.

Tax Sale Notice. 2 pages (newspaper), 1906.

Tax Sale. 1 volume, 1902-1906.

Cash Record (Revenues). 113 pages, 1905-1907.

Sheriffs' Costs (Disbursements). 90 pages, 1908-1911 and 1913.

Tax Collections (Revenues). 1 volume, 1908.

Fees Charged and Received. 1 volume, 1902-1922.

OKLAHOMA HISTORICAL SOCIETY   *GENERAL REPOSITORIES*

   Journals (2). 1 volume, 1903-1905.

   Ledger (General). 2 volumes, 1915-1935.

   Quarterly Reports. 1 volume, 1904-1907.

   School District Bond Register. 1 volume, 1902-1915.

   School District Bond Register, District Number 1 (Hobart). .2 cubic foot, 1902-1950.

   Tax Collections, Daily Registers, Townships. 3 volumes, 1903-1909.

   Tax Collections, Daily Register, School Districts. 1 volume, 1903-1904.

   Township Reports (Financial Statements) and Depository Bond Records. 1 volume, 1912-1915.

   Warrant Registers. 6 volumes, 1902-1941.

Logan County

   Memorandum, County Number 1, District Court. 1 volume, 1890-1891.

   United States Criminal Trial, Number 2 District Court, 1st District. 1893-1901.

   Logan County Sheriff Records (Fee). 1901-1903 and 1906-1907.

   Fee Record, Criminal. 1907-1909 and 1913-1916.

   Fee Record, Civil. 1907-1910 and 1914-1921.

Muskogee, City of

   City of Muskogee Mayors' Court. 1 volume, 1906-1907.

Osage County

   Naturalization Certificates, District Court. 1 volume, 1908-1920.

   Grand Juror Record 1 (Pawhuska, Oklahoma Territory). 1 volume, 1899-1906.

   Petit Jury Certificates. 1 volume, 1911-1913.

   Abstract of Tax Rolls, County Assessors. 1 volume, 1917-1920.

GENERAL REPOSITORIES   *OKLAHOMA HISTORICAL SOCIETY*

    Assessment Roll, Town of Black Dog. 1 volume, 1915.

    Chattel Mortgage Record (Index). 2 volumes, 1914-1917.

    Fee and Reception Record. 4 volumes, 1911-1919.

    Land Index, Books 1-3, Osage Abstract and Title Company. 3 volumes, no date.

    Lands, Numerical Index. 5 volumes, no date.

    Town Lots, Abstract of Title Osage Abstract and Title Company. 1 volume, 1906-1909.

    County Superintendents' Ledger. 1 volume, 1910-1913.

Payne County

    Justices' Docket, Cimarron Township. 1890-1903.

Pottawatomie County

    Guardians' Record, Number 1, County B. 1892-1898.

    Record of Court Proceedings, Number 1 County B. 1892-1897.

    Administrator and Guardian Annual and Final Reports and Inventories. 1894-1904.

    Trial Docket, Probate Court. 1897-1901.

    Administrators' Record. 1899-1902.

    Inventory and Appraisement. 1900-1904.

    Administrators' & Executors' Record 2. 1901-1907.

    Sales Bond Record 1. 1902-1911.

    Administrator and Guardian Reports. 1903-1909.

    Guardian Record, Number 3. 1 volume, 1903-1905.

    Administrators' Record, Number 3. 1 volume, 1903-1906.

OKLAHOMA HISTORICAL SOCIETY   GENERAL REPOSITORIES

Administrator and Guardian Sale Record. 1903-1908.

Administrators' Record, 3. 1 volume, 1905-1908.

Guardian Record, 4. 1 volume, 1906-1909.

Guardians' Annual Report, County Court, 4. 1 page, 1912.

Guardians' Bond Record, County Court, 1. 1 volume, 1917-1924.

Fee Book, Probate Court, 1. 1895-1904.

Reception Record, Number 2, Probate Court. 1902.

Fee Record, Probate Court, 3. 1902-1904.

Record of Fees, 3. 1903-1904.

Probate Fee Record, 5. 1 volume, 1903-1904.

Record of Fees, 6. 1 volume, 1904-1906.

Record of Fees, Probate Court, 8. 1905-1907.

Record of Fees, Probate Court, 9. 1 volume, 1906-1907.

United States Memoranda Docket, Number 1, 3rd District, Territory of Oklahoma, County B. 1891-1896.

General Index to United States Court Records, Number 2 Reverse, 3rd District, County B, Territory of Oklahoma. 1891-1907.

General Index to United States Court Record, Number 1 Direct, 3rd District, County B, Territory of Oklahoma. 1892-1897.

Indictment Record Number 1, District Court, 3rd Judicial District. 1892-1904.

Miscellaneous Record, Number 1, District Court, County B, 3rd Judicial District. 1895-1896.

Civil Minute Book 2 (and Criminal). 1897-1900.

United States Journal Number 1 (3rd Judicial District). 1897-1899.

Indictment Record, 2. 1 volume, 1897-1904.

GENERAL REPOSITORIES *OKLAHOMA HISTORICAL SOCIETY*

United States Journal, Number 2, 3rd District, Territory of Oklahoma, County B. 1899-1901.

Court Journal 3 (3rd Judicial District) Oklahoma Territory. 1901-1903.

United States Journal 4 (District Court, 3rd Judicial District). 1903-1905.

Civil Minutes, Number 3. 1900-1904.

Minute Record 1, District Court. 1904-1905.

Indictment Record 3. 1 volume, 1904-1909.

United States Journal 6 (3rd Judicial District). 1907.

Petit Juror Certificate Number 4, County B. 1892-1898.

Grand Jury Certificate, Number 2, County B. 1893-1898.

Witness Certificate, District Court, Number 1, County B. 1894-1898.

United States Appearance Docket, Number 3, 3rd District, Territory of Oklahoma, County B. 1892-1898.

United States Criminal Appearance Docket 2. 1896-1910.

Bankruptcy Docket. 1 volume, 1889-1907.

Civil Judgement Docket 1. 1891-1903.

Civil Trial Docket, Number 3. 1 volume, 1897-1898.

Civil Trial Docket, 5 (County Court). 1901-1903.

Civil Trial Docket 6. 1903-1905.

Civil Trial Docket. 1 volume, 1902-1906.

Civil Trial Docket, 7. 1906-1907.

Trial Docket Number 2, County B, Territory of Oklahoma. 1892-1895.

Trial Docket 1. 1894-1897.

Criminal Trial Docket, 3. 1 volume, 1895-1897.

Criminal Docket 2. 1897-1905.

Minute Docket Number 2. 1902-1908.

Judgement Docket Number 1, District Court, County B. 1892-1900.

United States Judgment Docket, Number 1. 1899-1906.

Subpoena Docket 1 (3rd District). 1899-1907.

Lunacy Record, Number 1, County B. 1 volume, 1893-1897.

Lunacy Record Number 2. 1903-1915.

Naturalization Record, Number 1, First Papers, County B, Oklahoma Territory. 1892-1896.

Naturalization Record, Number 1, Second Papers, County B, Oklahoma Territory. 1893-1902.

Citizenship Record, 1. 1903-1906.

Naturalization Service, Petition and Record, Volume 1, Numbers 1-100. 1919-1929.

Index to Claims, 2.

Record of Receipts and Expenditures Number 1, County Clerk, County B. 1891-1896.

Accounts Filed, Warrants Issued, Number 1, County B. 1892-1896.

Clerks' School Warrant Book, Number 1, County B. 1892-1897.

Cash Book 1, Clerk, County B, Oklahoma Territory. 1892-1894.

Fee Record A, Clerk. 1895-1915.

Contribution Record, School Districts, Clerk. 1897.

Estray Record, Number 2. 1 volume, 1899-1918.

Daily Collection Register. 1900.

Bridge Record, 1. 1903-1911.

GENERAL REPOSITORIES *OKLAHOMA HISTORICAL SOCIETY*

County Clerk's Calendar of Claims. 1904-1908.

Record of Fees, 11. 1 volume, 1908-1909.

Miscellaneous Docket, 1. 1910-1921.

Notarial Bond Record, 4. 1911-1920.

Monthly Report Record, County Court, 1. 1913-1915.

Criminal Trial Docket, 5, County Court. 1911-1913.

Criminal Docket, E.D. Reasor, Justice, Shawnee Township. 1906-1908.

Sheriffs' Execution Docket, Number 1. 1891-1910.

Sheriffs' Fee Record, A. 1 volume, 1895-1896.

Expense Record, A, Sheriff. 1 volume, 1898-1914.

Sheriffs' Register of Tax Warrants, 3. 1903-1907.

Sheriffs' Record of Criminal Work. 1906-1913.

Sheriffs' Ledger, 1. 1 volume, 1905-1907.

Financial Records of County Treasurer. 1892-1898.

Civil Trial Docket, Number 1, Superior Court. 1909-1914.

Judgement and Sentence Record, Number 1, Superior Court. 1909-1914.

Civil Trial Docket Number 2, Superior Court, Shawnee, Oklahoma. 1911-1914.

Swanson County

Assessment Rolls, Otter Creek Township and Cold Springs City. 1 volume, 1911.

Assessment Rolls, Hunter Township. 1 volume, 1911.

Deputy Sheriffs' Fee Record. 1 volume, 1911-1915.

Justice Official Bond Record. 1 page, 1911.

OKLAHOMA HISTORICAL SOCIETY   GENERAL REPOSITORIES

    Sheriffs' Fee Record (Criminal). 1 volume, 1911.

    Treasurers' Warrant Register. 1 volume, 1910-1911.

Normal Institute Records

    Book Number 2. Names of students, etc., 1905-1908.

    Book Number 1. Names of students, etc., 1894.

State Election Board, Oklahoma Museum of Election History (Oklahoma City, OK 73105)

Adair County

    Precinct Register. 1 volume, 1916-1920.

Blaine County

    Precinct Register. 1 volume, 1916-1932.

Carter County

    Minutes. 1 volume, 1908.

Choctaw County

    Abstract of Votes Cast. 1 volume, 1914-1936.

    County Register. 1 volume, 1916-1926.

Cleveland County

    County Register. 1 volume, 1916.

Coal County

    Abstract of Votes Cast. 1 volume, 1912-1940.

    County Register. 1 volume, 1916-1920.

Creek County

    Notice Establishing Precincts. 1 volume, 1918.

GENERAL REPOSITORIES *STATE ELECTION BOARD*

Record of Candidates for Nomination. 1 volume, 1912 and 1922.

Custer County

   Precinct Register. 1 volume, 1916-1920.

Dewey County

   Election Returns. 2 volumes, 1892-1907.

   Election Record. 1 volume, 1918-1950.

   Precinct Register. 1 volume, 1919-1931.

Ellis County

   Map (school district). 1 volume, 1900.

Garfield County

   Map (territory, railroads, etc.). 6 volumes, 1883-1911.

Grant County
   County Register. 1 volume, 1916-1924.

Greer County

   Precinct Register. 9 volumes, 1916-1950.

Kingfisher County

   Election Returns. 1 volume, 1890-1904.

   Election Record. 3 volumes, 1916-1952.

   Precinct Register. 3 volumes, 1916-1947.

Latimer County

   Claim Register. 1 volume, 1911-1922.

LeFlore County

   Election Returns. 1 volume, 1907-1938.

STATE ELECTION BOARD   *GENERAL REPOSITORIES*

Lincoln County

    Election Record. 1 volume, 1911-1938.

    County Register. 1 volume, 1916-1930.

    Precinct Register. 1 volume, 1916-1922.

Major County

    County Register. 1 volume, 1916-1938.

Marshall County

    Abstract of Votes Cast. 1 volume, 1912-1962.

Mayes County

    Minutes. 1 volume, 1908-1934.

Murray County

    Abstract of Votes Cast. 1 volume, 1920.

Muskogee County

    County Register. 1 volume, 1916.

Noble County

    County Register. 2 volumes, 1916-1934.

    Precinct Register. 3 volumes, 1916-1952.

    Register Book (for City of Glenrose). 1 volume, 1916-1938.

Nowata County

    Election Record. 1 volume, 1916-1952.

    County Register. 1 volume, 1916-1920.

    Precinct Register. 2 volumes, 1916-1954.

GENERAL REPOSITORIES *STATE ELECTION BOARD*

Pawnee County

    Precinct Register. 1 volume, 1918-1934.

Payne County

    Election Record. 2 volumes, 1916-1919.

Pontotoc County

    County Register. 1 volume, 1916.

Pottawatomie County (County B)

    Election Returns. 1 volume, 1892-1932.

Roger Mills County

    Election Returns. 1 volume, 1894-1902 and 1920.

    Election Record. 1 volume, 1916-1952.

    Copy of Ballot. 1 volume, 1894-1902.

    Precinct Boundary Line Record. 1 volume, 1919-1964.

    Precinct Register. 5 volumes, 1916-1938.

Rogers County

    Precinct Boundary Line Record. 1 volume, 1909-1946.

Sequoyah County

    County Register. 1 volume, 1916-1940.

Tillman County

    Minutes. 1 volume, 1910-1927.

Wagoner County

    County Register. 1 volume, 1916-1932.

STATE ELECTION BOARD   *GENERAL REPOSITORIES*

Washita County

    Precinct Register. 1 volume, 1916-1952.

University of Oklahoma, Western History Collections (Norman, OK 73019)

Fairland, Oklahoma: City Records Collection

    The following records are in small quantities with each listing containing less than .33 cubic foot.

    Correspondence. Concerns city indebtedness, 1933-1936.

    File of City Ordinances.

    Financial Record Book. 1912-1926.

    Monthly Balance Ledgers (2).

    Water Bonds, Electric Light Bonds, and Sinking Funds Day Book.

    Miscellaneous Receipt Book. 1933.

    Treasurers' Balance Book. 1925.

    Water Department Audit. 1933.

    Treasurers' Warrant Register. 1913-1935.

    Treasurers' Settlement Book.

    City Warrants and Accounts.

    Canceled Checks. 1930-1937.

    Sales Tokens.

    License Register. 1918.

    Treasurers' Report. 1925.

    Collection Register. 1921-1926.

    Account Book. 1912-1913.

GENERAL REPOSITORIES *WESTERN HISTORY COLLECTIONS*

Meter Deposit Record.

Warrants. 1930-36.

Fort Gibson: Records of the First National Bank

Town Treasurers' Monthly Report. 1 volume, May 1923 - January 1926.

Treasurers' Record (Muskogee County). 1 volume, December 1908 - May 1909.

Logan County Road Record Collection

Complete Road Record. Citizens of townships of Logan County, Oklahoma Territory, made application for permission to construct roadways, includes signatures of county surveyor and chairman of county board of commissioners, and maps drawn by applicants of road routes, 1 ledger, 1896-1905.

Miami, Oklahoma: City Records Collection

Minute Records Books. 8 books, 1899-1938.

Ordinance Records. 7 books, 1895-1949.

Nowata County Records Collection

Civil and Criminal Dockets. 19 ledgers, 1909-1939.

Applications for Homesteaders' Exemption Taxes. 8 books, 1937.

School District Valuation. 1 book, 1909.

Tax Assessment Lists. Arranged by township, 271 books, 1909-1939.

Agricultural Statistics. .5 cubic foot, 1910-1913.

Quapaw, Oklahoma: City Records Collection

The following records are in small quantities with each listing containing less than .33 cubic foot.

Township Ledger. 1 book, 1917-1919.

Minutes of the Board of Trustees. 1931-1938.

WESTERN HISTORY COLLECTIONS *GENERAL REPOSITORIES*

    Correspondence with the Federal Works Agency. 1945.

    Occupational License Certificates. 1925-1927.

    Water Consumers' Contracts. 1919-1920.

Shumard, Evelyn H. Collection

    Minutes of the Incorporated Town of Sapulpa, Indian Territory. .33 cubic foot, May 16, 1898 - October 16, 1902.

Welch, Oklahoma: Town Records Collection

    Criminal Docket. 1 book, 1899-1909.

    Minutes of Meetings of the Board of Trustees of Welch. 1 book, 1911-1926.

Womack, John Collection

    Cleveland County

    Saloon Liquor Applications, Petitions and Licenses. .33 cubic foot, 1896-1909.

    Claims (Treasurer, Assessor, etc.). 7 cubic feet, 1890-1928.

    The following records are in small quantities with each listing containing less than .33 cubic foot.

    Tax Warrants Collected by Sheriff. 1907.

    Sheriffs' Quarterly Reports. 1907-1910.

    Bonds. 1899-1912.

    Coroners' Reports. 1902-1907.

    Appointments, Oaths and Resignations. 1895-1912.

    Estrays. 1902-1919.

    Erroneous Assessments. 1896-1913.

    Justice of the Peace Reports. 1907-1910.

    Register of Deeds Reports. 1900-1909.

Railroad Assessments. 1891-1911.

Road Petitions. 1893-1911.

Treasurers' Reports. 1892 and 1901-1909.

School Bonds. 1899 and 1903-1906.

Judges' Records. 1907-1912.

Surveyor's Report. 1895.

Chattel Mortgage Data. 1891, 1892, 1915, 1916 and 1924.

Bridge Blueprints. 1909-1911.

Tax Assessment. 1892-1893 and 1900-1911.

Tax Assessor Appointment and Resignations. 1900-1906.

District Clerk Reports. 1910.

Tax Certificates. 1894-1901.

Statement of Assessment. 1894-1902.

Apportionments. 1899-1907.

Miscellaneous records of towns of Noble and Stella, and townships of Canadian, Case, Moore, Lexington, Little River and Liberty.

www.ingramcontent.com/pod-product-compliance
Lightning Source LLC
Chambersburg PA
CBHW071711160426
43195CB00012B/1648